THE COMPLETE BOOK OF SPICES

THE COMPLETE BOOK OF SPICES

by Ellen Freke

NEW BURLINGTON BOOKS

This book is dedicated

with thanks to my husband,

for his amazing patience and numerous cups of tea;

my dear friend Jean Card, for her incredible help, support, and enthusiasm;

Deborah O'Shea, for her imaginative ideas and beautiful decorations;

and especially my son Timothy, for his encouragement

and hard work editing this manuscript.

A QUINTET BOOK

Published by New Burlington Books
6 Blundell Street
London N7 9BH

ISBN 1-86155-172-X

This book was designed and produced by
Quintet Publishing Limited
6 Blundell Street
London N7 9BH

Creative Director: Richard Dewing
Art Director: Silke Braun
Designer: Rita Wüthrich
Senior Editor: Sally Green
Editor: Lisa Cussons
Photographer: Philip Wilkins

Typeset in Great Britain by
Central Southern Typesetters, Eastbourne
Manufactured in Singapore by
United Graphics Pte Ltd
Printed in China by Leefung-Asco Printers Ltd

CONTENTS

INTRODUCTION

"Awake, O North wind, and come, thou South; Blow upon my Garden, that the spices thereof may flow out."

Song of Solomon

Above *Spices are the seeds, fruits, roots, or flowers of plants. Nutmeg, for example, is the seed of the evergreen tree,* Myristica fragrans.

To think of spices is to conjure up the magic of the Orient. Although now familiar, they retain something of the mystery of their exotic heritage. Spices have become a symbol of adding zest and interest to just about anything, which is why we talk of "adding spice to your love-life" and "the spice of life." Without spices, cooking would not be such a rich and varied art. Their tastes and aromas combine to create a kaleidoscope of exotic flavors to delight the palate.

Spices were first used in their indigenous countries to transform what was an otherwise monotonous diet of local foods and badly preserved meats into a splendid array of gastronomic possibilities. As they have spread across the globe, they have become part of the world's culinary traditions and have helped create the vast spectrum of dishes available today. They have also made their way into some of the great liqueurs of the world, as well as being used in perfumes, and cosmetics such as soaps, skin creams, and breath-fresheners.

WHAT IS SPICE?

Spices are the seeds, fruits, barks, roots, or flowers of plants. Cardamom and nutmeg are seeds, for example, allspice and black pepper are fruits, cinnamon and cassia are barks, ginger and turmeric are roots, while cloves and saffron are derived from flowers. Unlike herbs, which grow in temperate zones, spices grow in the tropics. All the most important spices originate in the Orient, except allspice, vanilla, and capsicums such as chilies, which are indigenous to Central America. Some plants, such as dill, are both herbs and spices, where the seeds are regarded as a spice and the leaves as an herb.

The characteristic flavors of spices come from the essential oils that are concentrated in the spice through drying, helping them keep their aroma and taste for up to eighteen months. All spices are best ground as required, otherwise they will lose their flavor. Unlike herbs, they have little nutritional value, but, as well as adding taste, they also stimulate appetite and, therefore, the gastric juices that aid digestion.

Left *A wonderful spectrum of colors and aromas. Spices have spread across the globe to become part of the world's culinary traditions.*

NOT A MODERN COMMODITY

Spices have been used since ancient times. They are mentioned in the ancient Hindu scriptures called the Vedas, ancient Egyptian papyruses, and the Old Testament. The Queen of Sheba ruled over part of the Incense Route through southern Arabia to the Mediterranean and met with King David to develop the spice trade, which created much of his wealth. Although it was not until the Roman conquests that western countries discovered their culinary possibilities, spices have always been believed to have healing and magical qualities. They have been used to cast spells, as incense in religious rites, to embalm corpses, to add aroma to perfumes, and as aphrodisiacs. Their origins in the mystical East have made them the subject of endless myths and legends, many deliberately concocted by traders to protect their knowledge of where they actually purchased their valuable supplies. The ancient historian Herodotus relates that cinnamon was believed to come from gigantic limestone cliffs in Ethiopia, guarded by huge birds that nested there. In reality cinnamon originated in China, but this deliberate lie protected Arab merchants' monopoly on the spice until the 4th century AD.

LUCRATIVE TRADE

Below Pepper being gathered in the kingdom of Quilon, Livre des Merveilles, 15th century.

The word spice comes from the Latin species, meaning a commodity of value and distinction. During their long and fascinating history, spices have often been more valuable than gold or precious stones, and the trade in spices has been an extraordinarily influential factor in history. Empires have risen due to wealth from spices, and fallen when they lost their hold on these highly prized commodities. Men have risked their lives to explore the world in search of new routes to reach spice-growing countries, and to discover new spices. Wars have been fought to control their production, and huge numbers of native people have been enslaved to cultivate them.

When the crusaders returned from Palestine in the 12th century the spice trade began to flourish in earnest. The Renaissance, which sowed the seeds of modern Western culture, was built on the wealth made from trading spices in Venice and Genoa. The British East India Company, founded in 1600 to trade in spices after the defeat of the Spanish Armada, was to become the most powerful economic force in history, complete with its own armies, navies, currencies, and territories. It founded Hong Kong and Singapore, once held Napoleon captive, and laid the foundations for the corporate structure of present day capitalism.

THE EARLY SPICE MERCHANTS

During the first and second millennia BC, the spice trade was dominated by Arabia, whose merchants brought these precious commodities from East to West.Sri Lanka became an important meeting place between Arabic and Chinese traders, from where spices spread throughout the known world as it was then. When Alexander the Great expanded the Greek Empire as far as India in the 4th century BC, he discovered a direct trading route to the Orient, which was to break the dominance of Arabia. The city of Alexandria, which he founded in Egypt, became a busy, flourishing, and important spice-trading center.

In Alexander's wake, the Romans, fed up with paying exorbitant Arabian prices, dominated spice trading. After the fall of their Empire, the rising Islamic world took control of the market. The Arab prophet Muhammad, the founder of Islam, was himself a spice trader.

During the Dark Ages, the availability of spices in Europe declined dramatically. They became prohibitively expensive and were used almost exclusively in monasteries, mainly for medicinal purposes. It was not until the Crusades brought new contact with the Middle East that spices began to be more widely available, and by the time of the Fourth Crusade in 1204, the spice trade was again flourishing. Venice, in particular, became an important center, especially for pepper, holding a monopoly of trade with the Near East, Sri Lanka, the East Indies, and Cathay.

THE SPICE ROUTES

The great wealth that could be accumulated by trading in spices inspired many powerful European countries to find new trading routes to the East. In 1487, the Portuguese found a way to India by rounding the Cape of Good Hope. From there they opened up trading routes to China and farther east to Japan which was then virtually unknown. Lisbon became the most important spice port in Europe.

It was at about this time that Christopher Columbus persuaded the Spanish that he could reach India by sailing west across the Atlantic and accidentally discovered the "New World," mistakenly calling the Caribbean Islands the West Indies. Here he made history by becoming the first Westerner to experience the burning taste of chilies, which were previously not known by the inhabitants of the "Old World." Eventually in 1520 Spanish ships, commanded by the Portuguese adventurer, Ferdinand Magellan (1480?–1521), did arrive in the Pacific via the Straits that now bear his name, to reach the spice centers of the East. The same route was followed by England's Sir Francis Drake (1540/3–1590), who returned home with his ship, the *Golden Hind*, heavily laden with cloves.

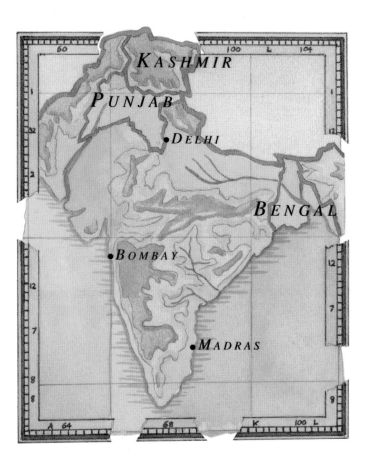

Above India is the principal producer of spices, exporting 70,000 tons of mainly pepper, chilies, turmeric, ginger, and of course curry powder. It accounts for about 20% of the world market.

THE SPICE WARS

There followed a brutal struggle to dominate the lucrative spice trade, mainly between the English, Portuguese, and the Dutch, known as the "Spice Wars." In 1595, successful voyages to the East Indies by the Dutch encouraged them to force up the price of pepper in England. This provocative act prompted London merchants to form the British East India Company by special charter from Queen Elizabeth I, to develop the British spice trade. The Dutch responded with the Dutch East India Company, and as the Portuguese power decreased, the battle for supremacy of the spice trade became primarily between these two great companies: an economic and armed struggled that lasted for two centuries, ending with Britain in control of India and Sri Lanka, and the Dutch in control of the East Indies.

In the 17th and 18th centuries, the history of spices is a bloody one. Not only were there wars over the centers of spice production, but the indigenous peoples were brutally oppressed and enslaved in order to cultivate the crops. The Dutch tried to limit production of a particular spice to one island only, in an attempt to maintain their monopoly on production by preventing it being grown elsewhere, with the death penalty imposed for exporting seeds. Pierre Poivre, who had originally been a missionary, eventually smuggled 3,000 nutmeg seeds, along with other spices and tropical trees, to Mauritius, an island in the Indian Ocean. Thereafter spices were grown in the tropics all over the world, and the Dutch monopoly was broken.

By the late 18th century, the United States began to enter the spice business in earnest, with trade between Salem and the East creating many millionaires, and New York, Baltimore, and San Francisco becoming important centers.

A MODERN INDUSTRY

Today, the spice trade is still an extremely lucrative business. As a result of the spread of spices, no one country has been able to maintain a monopoly on any particular spice though India remains the principal producer, with about 20% of the world market, yearly exporting 70,000 tons of mainly pepper, chilies, turmeric, ginger, and, of course, curry powder.

Indonesia is the next largest producer, cultivating cloves, nutmegs, peppers, vanilla, and ginger. The other major producers are Brazil, Madagascar, and Malaysia. The United States is the major importer of spices, followed by Germany, Japan, and France. This trade involves about 350,000 tons of spices a year, and is worth in the region of $1.5 billion.

Black pepper is, unsurprisingly, by far the most popular spice, with the amounts traded on the world market being larger than all the other spices added together. Chilies and cardamom are the next most common.

Through world trade, spices have become much cheaper and no longer the preserve of a rich, privileged elite, allowing everyone to enjoy one of the great natural riches of the world.

The Use of Spices

Healing Spices

Above right *In folk medicine, a particular spice was regarded as a cure for an illness to which its color and shape suggested a correspondence. The phallic-looking clove, Eugenia caryophyllus, was naturally an aphrodisiac.*

Spices have been used medicinally since Ancient Times. In 270 BC, Shen Nung of Cathay mentions Cassia as a Remedy in his Pen Ta'ao Ching, the earliest known Herbal, a Book expounding the Medicinal Properties of Plants. Spice cures were subsequently set down in Herbals from Ancient Assyria and Sumer. The Egyptian "Ebers Papyrus" (circa 1550 BC) lists Anise, Caraway, Cassia, Coriander, Cardamom, Mustard, Sesame, Fenugreek, Saffron, and Poppy Seeds as Spices used in Healing. The greatest ancient Greek physicians and scientists, such as Herodotus, Theophrastus, and Dioscorides, remark on their medicinal properties, while Hippocrates, regarded as "the father of medicine," talks of saffron, cinnamon, coriander, pepper, and ginger as "useful plants." In 80 BC, Crateuas, the physician to Mithridates, King of Pontus, concocted a remarkable remedy for poison using all 36 of the spices known at the time, mixed together with honey and wine. In his book Natural History, the Roman writer Pliny sees it from a slightly different angle, claiming that spices can be used to treat nearly everything (Crateuas would have said all spices taken together could do the same).

The great 10th-century Muslim physician Avicenna (980–1037), who revolutionized medieval Western medicine with his Canon of Medicine, is credited with discovering the distillation process for extracting oils from herbs and spices.

Plague Relief

Although ironically it was most probably rats living aboard ships bringing spices from the East that also brought the dreaded plague to Europe, sufferers turned to spices for relief. They drank juniper wine and saffron tea, bathed using sponges soaked in clove and cinnamon extract, and wore nosegays—nosebags of aromatic and antiseptic spices to help prevent infection. The influential 17th-century herbalist and astrologer, the Englishman Nicholas Culpeper, believed that the essential oil of spices could cure all kinds of ailments.

In folk medicine, the so-called "Doctrine of Signatures" was applied to spices, by which a particular spice was regarded as a cure for an illness to which its color or shape suggested a correspondence. For instance, yellow saffron was thought to be good for jaundice, and the phallic-looking clove was naturally an aphrodisiac.

Today, spices are not widely used in medicine, except in ancient Hindu Ayurvedic cures, still popular in India.

Can Spices be Harmful?

While there is no real evidence to support it, hot spices are sometimes thought to cause the skin to break out. Eating very spicy food can stimulate perspiration, which is why those living in hot countries like India favor dishes like curries. The perspiration evaporates on the skin, creating a temporary cooling effect, but not rashes or other outbreaks. However, spices may also stimulate the production of sebum, which, when combined with perspiration, can lead to blackheads.

It should be remembered that spices are also sometimes thought to cause ulcers. While some spices, such as pepper, cloves, and nutmeg, are known to inflame the intestinal lining, other non-irritating spices, although they may singe your tongue, will do no harm to your stomach. Obviously, if a spice is found to be an irritant, it should be avoided.

Healing spices can be used in many ways. The following: infusions, decoctions, ointments, poultices, fomentations, inhalants, and massage oils, are various forms of preparation. There are also some suggestions of particular spices that can be helpful to ease common ailments. For example, ginger is good for colds, while essential oils of many spices are beneficial for numerous ailments. It is always fun to experiment with using spices to treat common ailments, and many people have found them extraordinarily beneficial. However, it is extremely important to remember that, if the condition persists or is serious, you should always consult a doctor.

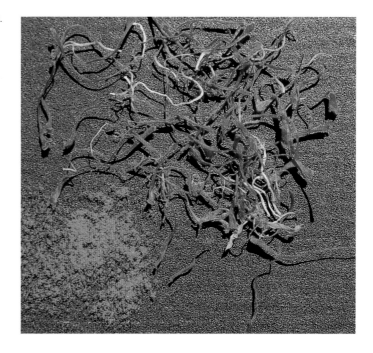

Below *Saffron, Crocus sativus, being yellow, was thought to be good for jaundice.*

METHODS OF PREPARATION

Infusions

Infusions are healing drinks. Pour 2½ cups boiling water over ¼ cup of the spice, and leave to brew for 5 minutes. Make sure that a lid is used, otherwise the healing powers will evaporate in the vapors. Strain, and drink the mixture.

A *poppy seeds* infusion with honey makes an excellent night-time drink for sleeplessness, while *lemon grass* is good for colds and flu.

Ointments

Float ¾ cup Vaseline in a saucepan of water. Stir in ¾ cup dried spice and 3 tbsp beeswax. Leave for 1–1½ hours over low heat, then strain into containers while still hot.

When cold and solidified, apply as needed.

Mustard ointment is good for chilblains, while *galangal* ointment treats skin disorders.

Decoctions

Decoctions are another form of healing drink. Simmer 2 tbsp of a spice root or seeds with 3 cups water until the liquid is reduced by a third. Strain and drink the mixture.

Kaffir lime decoctions are good for coughs and colds, *pomegranate* helps dysentery, and *celery* treats rheumatism.

Use *Kaempferia galangal* to produce a mouthwash for abscesses, and *fenugreek* for a gargle to ease sore throats.

Poultices

Mix powdered spice with boiling water to form a hot paste. Wrap the paste in a muslin cloth, then apply externally to the body, making sure the poultice is as hot as can be born. Remove every 5 minutes, and, if necessary, reheat in a microwave or use new paste.

Mustard seed poultices stimulate the blood, while ear infections may be eased by a poultice of *caraway*. *Poppy seed* poultices help toothache when placed on the jaw.

Fomentations

Make a spice infusion or decoction, then let it cool. When cold, prepare another, and dip a towel in the hot liquid. wring it out, and apply externally to the painful area for a few minutes. Then dip another towel in the cold infusion or decoction and apply for a few minutes. Repeat, alternating between hot and cold.

Mustard fomentations are excellent for aches and pains, while cool *clove* fomentations make good eye pads.

Inhalants

Put 2 tsp of spice into 1¼ cups boiling water, and mix well. Position your head near to the bowl, and then cover both bowl and head with a towel to keep the steam in.

Inhale the steam deeply for a few minutes. Repeat as necessary until condition improves.

When suffering from a cold, try using warming **Ginger** inhalants.

Massage Oils

Adding a few drops of essential oil from a spice to a massage oil enhances the latter's soothing, healing, and aromatic qualities. Almond oil is an excellent carrier oil.

Suitable essential oils of spices include *dill* (for digestive problems and colic in children); *fennel* (for digestive problems); *ginger* (for nervous disorders); *juniper* (to help detoxify and cleanse); *black pepper* (to increase circulation); and *lemon grass* (for refreshment).

For a massage to aid digestion and colic, add 3 drops *essential oil of dill* and 3 drops *essential oil of fennel* to 3 tbsp almond oil. For a refreshing and stimulating massage, add 1 drop *essential oil of pepper* and 3 drops *essential oil of lemon grass* to 3 tbsp almond oil. An aromatic and healing mixture can be made using *ginger* and *juniper*, which is good for the nervous system. Essential oils of spices are generally warming and stimulating, and if used too strongly can be irritating to the skin. When using these oils on someone with a sensitive skin, or on children, use half the recommended amount of essential oil.

Below *Spices make useful and exotic additions to massage oils; a few drops of essential oil of spice enhances their soothing and healing properties.*

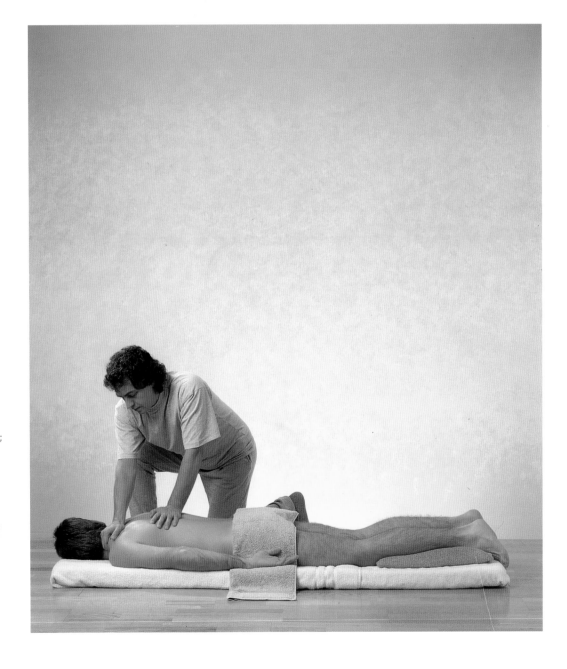

Spices in Food and Drink

GRINDING SPICES

IF YOU REQUIRE POWDERED SPICE, IT IS OFTEN BEST TO GRIND YOUR OWN SINCE THIS WILL GIVE THE MAXIMUM FLAVOR AND AROMA. FOR CENTURIES IN THE EAST, THEY HAVE BEEN GRINDING THEIR SPICE SEEDS WITH STONES, WHILE TRADITIONALLY A MORTAR AND PESTLE IS USED IN THE WEST. THIS IS HARD WORK, HOWEVER, AND ALMOST IMPOSSIBLE WITH SEEDS SUCH AS POPPY AND FENUGREEK. ELECTRIC MIXERS ARE GENERALLY NOT SUITABLE FOR GRINDING SPICES, ALTHOUGH KENWOOD NOW HAVE A SPICE GRINDER ATTACHMENT THAT IS PERFECT FOR THE JOB; A SMALL COFFEE GRINDER IS EQUALLY EFFECTIVE. THE HAND GRINDERS USED FOR HORSERADISH, OR A POPPY SEED GRATER, ARE ALSO VERY EFFECTIVE, THOUGH CAN BE SOMEWHAT MORE DIFFICULT TO OBTAIN.

SPICED OILS & VINEGARS

To add flavor to cooking, spices can be added to oil. Place spices in a bottle with a neck large enough to take the whole spice, then cover with oil. Cork and leave for 2–3 days. Heated vinegar mixed with fresh spices will assume their flavors, and can be used to create wonderful salad dressings.

Hot Oil

Heat ½ cup vegetable oil in a small cast-iron pan over a medium heat. When the oil is hot, add 1½ tsp ground cayenne pepper or chili pepper. Stir once. Remove from heat, and allow to cool slightly. Strain and store in an airtight bottle. This is an orange-colored oil popular in Chinese cooking; use it in very small quantities to dribble into soups and sauces.

Spiced Vinegar

Empty a bottle of wine or cider vinegar into a saucepan. Add 1 tsp each of peppercorns, whole cloves, ground ginger, and celery seeds, plus 1 cinnamon stick, 1 dried chili, and 2 tsp sugar. Bring to a boil, and then simmer for 3 minutes. Cool and bottle without straining.

Fragrant Vinegar

Put 1 heaped tbsp of the fresh or dried spice leaves into a jar. Gently heat 2½ cups white vinegar, and then pour onto the leaves. Screw on the lid, then leave in a warm place for 2 weeks. Strain and bottle.

Cayenne Vinegar

Mix 5 cups vinegar and 3 tbsp cayenne pepper in a bottle. Leave for 1 month, shaking the bottle daily. Strain and bottle.

Chili Vinegar

Cut 50 fresh chilies into halves. Boil 2½ cups good pickling vinegar, leave it to become cold, then pour it over the chilies. Keep the mixture in an airtight container to store until needed, then bottle and use.

SPICED HONEY

TASTY SPICED HONEYS CAN BE PREPARED USING SPICES SUCH AS VANILLA, CINNAMON, CARDAMOM, AND ALLSPICE. TRY THEM TO LIVEN UP YOUR TOAST AND HONEY, OR TO MAKE EXTRA WARMING NIGHT-TIME DRINKS.

Cardamom Honey Dressing

A delicious dressing for fruit salads, melons, or waffles.

Ingredients

1¼ cups clear honey

2 tbsp lemon juice

a few drops orange-flower water

½ tsp cracked cardamom seed

Preparation

Beat honey in a mixer until light in color.

Gradually add in the lemon juice and orange-flower water. Stir in cardamom seed.

Keep in an airtight jar.

Honey Ginger

Ginger honey is good poured over melon.

Ingredients

1½–2½ -inch cube fresh ginger root

1 lemon

2tbsp honey

2 cups water

Preparation

Peel the ginger, and roughly chop two-thirds of it. Remove several strips of peel from the lemon.

Mix the water and honey, then add in the slices of lemon and chopped ginger. Bring to the boil, then simmer for 7 minutes.

Remove and discard lemon and ginger.

Slice the remaining ginger as finely as possible, then cut into small threads. Remove another piece of peel from the lemon, and cut it as small as possible.

Add the ginger and lemon bits to the syrup, and simmer for 10 minutes. Cool.

Add some lemon juice before use.

SPICED BUTTER

BUTTER ROLLED IN SPICE WILL TAKE ON A NEW, SPICY FLAVOR. DELICIOUS SPICE BUTTERS CAN BE MADE WITH SPICES SUCH AS CAYENNE, MUSTARD, JUNIPER, SAFFRON, CHILI, PEPPER, PAPRIKA, AND DILL. USE IN SANDWICHES OR ADD A KNOB TO VEGETABLES – IT MAKES ALL THE DIFFERENCE!

Mustard Butter

Ingredients

1 cup unsalted butter

3 tbsp mustard powder

freshly ground white pepper

lemon juice

Preparation

Mix the mustard powder with the lemon juice, adding water if necessary.

Soften the butter, then beat in the mustard. Add the pepper, and mix.

Form into a sausage shape, and chill until required.

Cut into slices to serve.

SPICY DRINKS

SPICES PLAY AN ESSENTIAL PART IN FLAVORING SOME OF THE GREATEST LIQUEURS, SUCH AS OUZO, KÜMMEL, BENEDICTINE, CURAÇAO AND PERNOD. ADDING SPICES TO BOTH ALCOHOLIC AND NONALCOHOLIC DRINKS IS A WAY OF MAKING THEM SOMETHING SPECIAL. THE FOLLOWING ARE POPULAR RECIPES TO DELIGHT THE PALATE.

ALCOHOLIC DRINKS

Below Calvados punch makes a delightfully warming drink which is very easy to make. Cinnamon sticks are not only useful in cooking, but also make an attractive decorative garnish.

Right Mulled wine is a classic winter warmer perfect for Christmas festivities. It's a real celebration of the warming qualities of spices.

Calvados Punch

Ingredients

4 cups apple juice

1 cup ginger ale

2–3 cinnamon sticks

1 cup calvados

water

Preparation

Mix the apple juice, water, ginger ale, and cinnamon sticks in a saucepan over a low heat.

Pour the calvados equally into two glasses.

Bring the juice mix almost to simmering point, then pour through a sieve to catch the sticks and pour into the glasses.

Garnish with a cinnamon stick, if desired.

Mulled Wine

A deliciously warming winter drink.

Ingredients

1¼ cups water

½ cup sugar

4 cloves

2-inch stick cinnamon

2 lemons, finely sliced

1 bottle red wine

1 orange or lemon, sliced, for decoration

Preparation

Put the water, sugar, and spices in a large saucepan and heat for 5 minutes.

Add the lemons, and leave to stand for 10 minutes.

Pour in the wine and reheat, but do not allow to boil.

Strain, and serve hot decorated with lemon or orange slices.

NONALCOHOLIC DRINKS

Spicy Sorrel Drink

A delicious, refreshing herb drink.

Preparation time 20 minutes. Cooking time 1 minute.

Serves 10

Ingredients

1lb fresh sorrel leaves or 4oz dry sorrel leaves

2 bay leaves

3 whole cloves

1 small cinnamon stick

2lb white sugar

Preparation

Put the sorrel and bay leaves, cloves, cinnamon, and sugar into a large saucepan. Pour hot water over to cover the leaves and boil for 1 minute only.

Remove the pan from the heat and leave to cool. Leave to stand overnight.

Next day, sieve out the leaves and spices and sweeten to taste, if necessary. Bottle and put 1 whole clove in each bottle.

Cap the bottles and leave to stand for 4 days. Chill and serve with ice cubes.

Ginger Beer

A homemade version of a very popular drink.

Preparation time 20 minutes. Cooking time 5 minutes.

Serves 6

Ingredients

4oz piece fresh gingerroot

juice of 1 lime or lemon

3 whole cloves

2lb sugar

5 pints water

Preparation

Peel the gingerroot and slice it thinly. Put the ginger slices, lime and lemon juice, cloves, and sugar in the cold water in a saucepan. Bring to a boil and boil for 5 minutes. Remove the pan from the heat and leave to stand overnight.

The next day, sieve and adjust to taste. Bottle the ginger beer, adding a whole clove to each bottle. Cap the bottles and leave them to stand for 5 days. Chill and serve with ice cubes.

SPICE TEAS

TEAS CAN BE MADE FROM MANY SPICES, SUCH AS FENNEL, CARAWAY, DILL, JUNIPER, CITRUS, ANISE, GINGER, CARDAMOM, CINNAMON, FENUGREEK, AND SESAME, EITHER ALONE OR IN COMBINATION WITH OTHER SPICES.

Ginger Tea

Peel a couple of 1-inch cubes of fresh ginger, and chop coarsely. Put in a pot with 3¾ cups water and 3 heaped tbsp honey. Bring to a boil. Cover, turn heat to low, and simmer for 25 minutes. Uncover, turn up heat slightly and leave for 15 minutes. Strain and serve.

Fenugreek Tea

Warm a small teapot and put 2 tsp fenugreek seeds into it. Pour on boiling water to just cover the seeds. Leave for 10 minutes or longer for the taste to develop. When wanted, pour in more boiling water, stir and serve with honey and lemon.

Hot Tea with Cardamom and Cinnamon

Put 2 tbsp black tea into a warm teapot. Add 6 cardamom pods and a 2-inch piece of cinnamon stick, then pour 5 cups boiling water over the top. Cover, and leave to steep for 4 minutes. Serve with milk, sugar, honey, lemon, or just plain.

Hot Tea with Anise

Put 4 tsp anise seeds into 3¾ cups boiling water. Cover, and steep for ten minutes. Strain, and bring to boil again. Warm a teapot, then put in 4 tsp black tea. Pour the boiling anise over the tea; cover, and leave for 3 minutes. Serve as above.

SPICE MIXTURES

SPICES COMPLEMENT EACH OTHER LIKE COLORS IN A PAINTING, BLENDING TOGETHER TO BRING OUT EACH OTHER'S FLAVORINGS. THE FOLLOWING SPICE MIXTURES ARE POPULAR CULINARY COMBINATIONS. WHEN USING NON-GROUND SPICES, YOU MAY LIKE TO COOK WITH THE PREPARED MIXTURE IN A SPICE BAG, WHICH CAN KEEP ALL THE SPICES TOGETHER AND ENSURE THEY ARE EASILY REMOVED BEFORE SERVING SO THAT NO UNWANTED BITS ARE LEFT IN THE DISH.

Making a Spice Bag

1 Take a piece of muslin, and cut a circle around a small plate. Use pinking shears to avoid the muslin unraveling.

2 Place the required spices for the meal into the center, then pull the sides up all around to make a little bag.

3 Secure firmly with thread or string. Leave a tail that will hang over the side of the saucepan so that the spice bag can be easily removed, but make sure it's not long enough to catch fire on a gas ring or hotplate.

4 Place the spice bag into the food while cooking. Bob it up and down occasionally to make sure spices are permeating the entire dish. Remove before serving. The bag can really only be used once.

2 cups sliced carrots

1 cup green beans, cut in julienne sticks

1½ tsp sugar

1 tsp salt

½ cup malt vinegar

Preparation

Put all spices into a spice bag.

Blanch the onions and carrots for 5 minutes, and the beans for 2 minutes, in salted boiling water. Drain thoroughly.

Put the vinegar, bag of pickling spices, vegetables, sugar and salt in non-metallic bowl. Cover and leave for 4 days.

Remove bag. Put vegetables into jars, with the liquid.

Pickling Recipe

Pickling spice is used for pickling all sorts of vegetables.

2 tbsp allspice or pimento

1 tbsp mustard seeds

2 tsp fennel seeds

2 tsp dill seeds

2 tsp bird's eye chilies

1 tsp whole cloves

2 tsp cinnamon bark, broken into small pieces

2 tbsp bay leaves, crushed

Ingredients

pickling spice (as mixture above)

6 cups boiling water

2 cups pickling onions

Curry Blend

Ingredients

4 tsp coriander

2 tsp cumin

2 tsp turmeric

1 tsp ginger

½ tsp chili powder

1 tsp cinnamon

¼ tsp cloves

1 tsp fenugreek

¼ tsp mustard powder

¼ tsp black pepper

Preparation

Use all powdered spices. Sieve spices if lumpy. Mix altogether and keep in an airtight jar.

Above *Probably the most well-known and popular use of spices is in curries. Try the classic curry blends or experiment to suit your taste.*

North Indian Garam Masala

Garam masala means "warm spice blend," and is used toward the end of cooking. It is an Indian mixture used most commonly in curries, as well as in salads. There are various recipes of this mixture, coming from different parts of India. If you prefer to use a ready-mixed commercial powder, the flavor will be much improved if the powder is heated very gently for 5 minutes in a dry frying pan before use.

Ingredients

1 tbsp cardamom seeds
1-inch stick cinnamon
1 tsp whole cumin seeds
1 tsp whole cloves
1 tsp black peppercorns
⅓ of a nutmeg, grated

Preparation

Grind all the seeds in coffee grinder. Store in airtight jar away from sunlight and heat.

Other Spice Mixes

Chinese Five-Spice Star anise, fagara, fennel, cassia, cloves. A Chinese blend used in Asian cooking such as bean curd with mushrooms and peanuts covered with *hoisin* sauce.

Malayan Blend Chili, tamarind, coconut, galangal, candlenuts, lime leaf. As the name suggests, this combination of spices comes from Malaysia, and it is used in dishes such as eggplant stewed in coconut milk.

Cajun Mix Paprika, chili, cumin, mustard, oregano. A blend of spices used in Mexican fried beans and other Central American dishes.

Pumpkin Pie Mix Cinnamon, allspice, nutmeg, ginger. A Thanksgiving favorite.

Chat Masala Asafetida, ajowan, cumin, mint, cayenne, ginger, mango, pomegranate seeds. An Indian mix used for salads such as *gujarati* (cucumber and peanut salad).

Quatre-épices Black peppercorns, cloves, ginger, nutmeg, cinnamon. A French combination used in dishes such as red cabbage with chestnuts.

Zahtar Sumac, roasted sesame seeds, thyme. Used to flavor meatballs and hamburgers.

Harrissa Red chili, coriander seeds, caraway, garlic, cumin, mint in olive oil. This is a Tunisian mix which is used to flavor any tangy *couscous* (a steamed semolina dish prepared with vegetables and meat).

Dyeing Using Spices

SPICES SUCH AS POMEGRANATE, PAPRIKA, CINNAMON, SUMAC, CAYENNE, POPPY FLOWERS, CASSIA, AND TAMARIND LEAVES CAN ALL BE USED AS ATTRACTIVE NATURAL DYES. SAFFRON AND TURMERIC, HOWEVER, ARE THE EASIEST AND PROBABLY THE BEST SPICES TO USE FOR DYEING MATERIAL. YOU MAY LIKE TO EXPERIMENT BY DYEING A PIECE OF CLOTH WITH SAFFRON, AND THEN USING THE CLOTH TO MAKE AN AROMATIC SPICE SACHET (SEE PAGE 36). TURMERIC, WHICH IS MUCH CHEAPER THAN SAFFRON, CAN BE USED SIMILARLY.

1 Select a 12-inch x 12-inch piece of cloth. Muslin, cheesecloth, toweling, and cotton accept this dye beautifully. Nylon and satin dye to a paler yellow. Saffron dyes some blue materials green.

2 Place 2 teaspoons saffron into a bowl big enough to take the material to be dyed, and cover it with 2½ cups very hot, almost boiling water. (For larger lengths of material, use more water and more spice as required.) Stir until the powder has dissolved.

3 If you wish to "tie-dye" the material, bunch it into little knots and tie them tightly with string or thread. This will prevent the dye taking evenly, and create an attractive streaky effect.

4 Submerge the material in the dyeing liquid, making sure it is covered. Saffron can stain nearly everything, so wear rubber gloves. Press the material down for a while to make sure the color has penetrated. Leave for at least 4 hours; overnight is better, if possible.

5 Squeeze out material, and rinse well in cold water to remove excess dye and any powder that did not quite dissolve. Your cloth will now be a beautiful yellow color.

Above Spices for dyeing. From left to right: sumac, paprika, turmeric, cinnamon, and saffron.

Decorating with Spices

IN THE HOME

SPICES CAN CREATE NATURALLY BEAUTIFUL AND AROMATIC DECORATIONS. THEY CAN BE USED IMAGINATIVELY TO GIVE CHARACTER TO THE KITCHEN, IN AROMATIC BAGS TO SWEETEN CUPBOARDS AND DRAWERS, AND TO MAKE ORIGINAL GIFTS, AND TRADITIONAL CHRISTMAS DECORATIONS.

Decorated Spice Drawers

A little set of drawers is a practical way to keep your spices, and will make an attractive addition to the kitchen. As the drawers may not be entirely airtight, it may be best to store the spices in small plastic bags within each drawer. The set of drawers can be decorated with spices to both mark each drawer and to make an unusual decoration.

You Will Need
a set of drawers
masking tape
a small lid to draw around
pencil
glue
paintbrush
a selection of spices;
for example, ground ginger, dill weed, ground lemon grass, cayenne pepper, cumin, celery seed

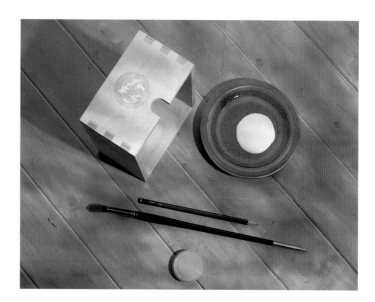

1 Draw around the lid in the center of the face of one of the drawers and fill the circle with glue. Be careful not to go over the edges.

2 Pour your selected spice onto the glue circle, press into place and then pour off the excess. Paint the rest of the drawer face with glue.

3 Pour another spice, in a contrasting color, onto the entire surface, press down and then pour off the excess. Repeat with the other drawers.

Alternatives

Use drawers with knobs and stencil the names of the spices you want to keep inside onto the face of each drawer. "Paint" a line with glue on either side of the knob. Cover with the chosen spice and shake off.

Decorative Spice Bottle

A bottle or spaghetti holder filled with different layers of colored spices creates a beautifully colorful kitchen ornament which is very simple to make. For a more dramatic effect, try inserting a layer of rock salt between spices. This enhances the colors of the spices by adding a startling contrast.

> **1** Make a funnel by rolling the paper into a cone, with a hole at the narrow end, and tape it into shape. Make sure that the narrow opening fits into the mouth of the bottle.

You Will Need

attractive empty bottle

colorful spices

Good spices to use include star anise,

cloves, coriander, cayenne powder, cinnamon

powder, turmeric powder, black and white pepper corns,

yellow and blue poppy seeds, and mustard seeds.

paper

masking tape

> **2** Select a collection of colorful spices that combine attractively from the selection suggested. Choose one spice and pour it into the bottle to the depth required.

3 Gently shake the bottle a little to let the spice settle evenly, before repeating with the next spice, and so on until the bottle is filled with layers of color. If you are using a spaghetti holder, replace the cork.

4 Tie raffia and a spice decoration around the neck of the bottle. In this case a star anise has been used, but you could try chilis, vanilla pods, or dried fruit.

Alternatives

You can experiment with a wide variety of shapes and sizes of bottle and an equally wide variety of spice combinations. Use with or without rock salt.

Garland of Spices

A garland of spices is a beautiful and natural-looking decoration to hang in the kitchen, bringing a simple, rustic charm to the modern cooking area.

You Will Need
large needle
attractive thread or raffia
nutmegs
vanilla beans
various types of dried chilies* and/or fruit
liquorice sticks

*If you want to dry your own chilies, using a microwave is excellent and fast, stopping them going moldy or floppy. Use a slow-cook setting and check regularly until they are dried.

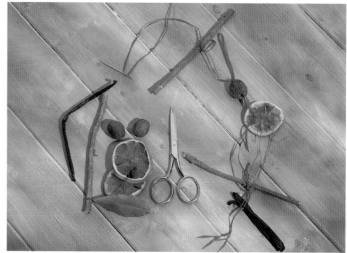

1 Select the combinations of beans and dried chilies and/or fruit you wish to use. Using a large needle, thread one thing after the other onto an attractive thread. Tie on the vanilla beans and liquorice sticks.

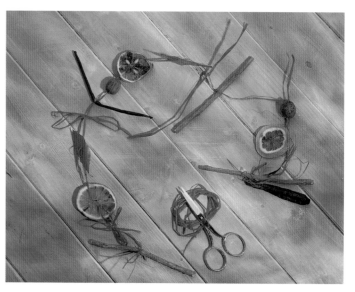

2 Having attached as many spices as desired, tie the ends of the thread together and hang from a nail on the wall.

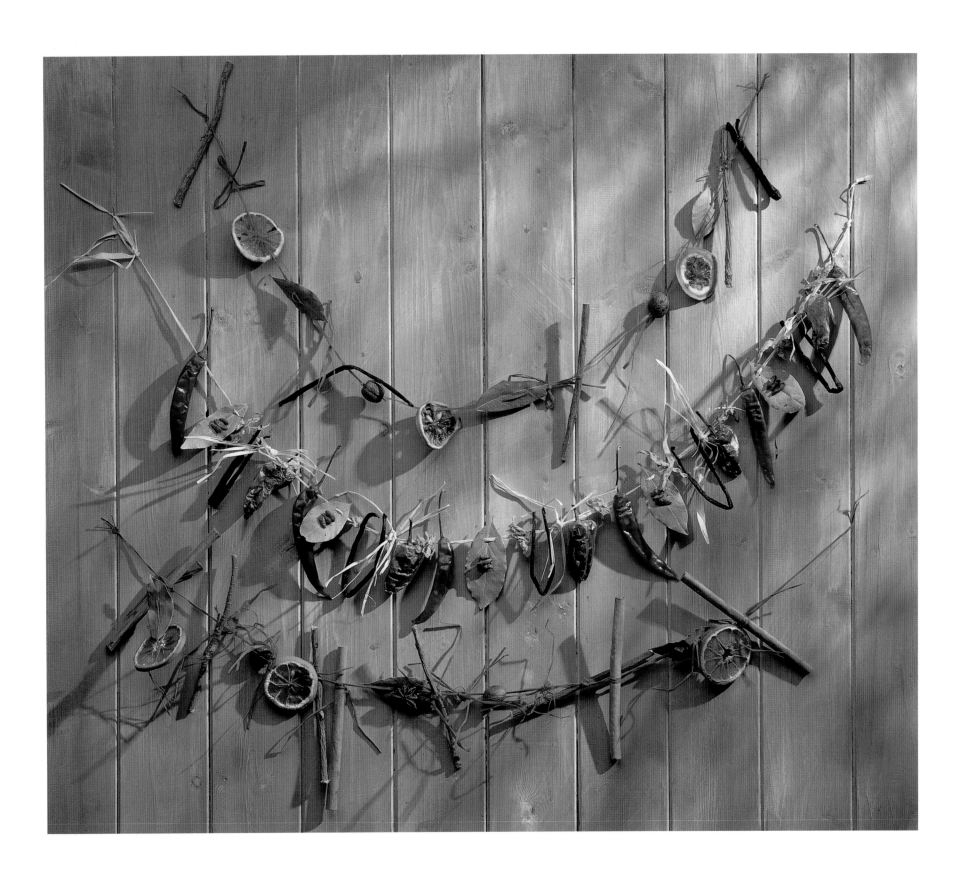

Potpourri

A bowl of potpourri makes a pretty and fragrant addition to any room. Try these two mixtures for springtime and Christmas, or, if you really like one, for all year round!

A light, refreshing, springtime potpourri mixture

2 oz caraway

2 oz cinnamon sticks

½ cup cardamom

½ cup fennel

2 marigold flowers

6 drops neroli essential oil

6 drops lemon grass essential oil

A rich potpourri mixture with an aroma of Christmas

2 oz myrtle leaves

1 oz cinnamon sticks

½ cup cloves

½ cup star anise

½ cup rosemary

⅓ cup juniper berries

⅓ cup black pepper

6 drops essential oil of frankincense

6 drops essential oil of orange

2 drops essential oil of cinnamon

2 drops essential oil of ginger

You Will Need

attractive basket or bowl

potpourri mixture

(refreshing springtime or rich potpourri)

1 Mix the potpourri ingredients by hand in a plastic bag, so that the mixture is well blended, adding the essential oils last. Shake the bag. Place in an attractive basket or bowl and display.

Drawstring Spice Bags

These drawstring spice bags look and smell delicious! Pamper yourself, or give as a charming gift. Ideal for hanging on a coat hanger inside a closet to keep the contents sweet-smelling. There are two spice mixtures to choose from, one for men and another for women.

You Will Need

white cotton

gingham fabric

felt

dressmaking pins

sewing machine

fabric glue

scissors

Spice mixture

Spice mixture for women

¼ oz vanilla pods

2 tbsp lemon grass

2 tsp juniper berries

Spice mixture for men

1 heaped tbsp cloves

1 tbsp allspice

¼ oz lime leaves

1 Cut a rectangle of gingham measuring 15 inches x 6 inches, and a strip of gingham 12 inches x 1 inch and fold the rectangle in half, then at the top of each short end fold down 2 inches, turn the raw edges of these turnings in again at ⅓ inch and pin into place. Sew a line along the bottom of the turning and then another ⅓ inch above that, to form a channel.

2 Fold with the right sides together and pin up the sides. Sew up the sides to the lower row of stitching on the turn-up.

4 Thread the drawstring through the channels, using a safety pin. Cut out a heart from the felt and glue onto the middle of the bag.

Alternatives

Use muslin, or another fine fabric for femininity. Sew sequins all over the bag. Appliqué tiny lace motifs in a pattern of your choice on the front of the bag. These charming, delicate little bags make perfect containers for the spice mixture for women. They'll also be appreciated as birthday, Valentine, or Mother's Day gifts.

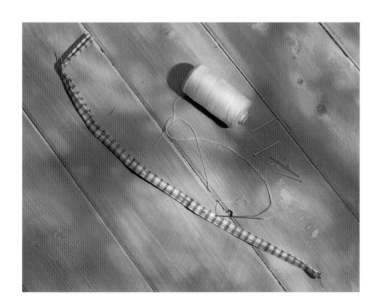

3 Fold the strip in half, along the length, folding in the raw edge, and slipstitch together. Press and iron to make insertion into the bag easier.

SPICE GIFTS

ONCE YOU HAVE BUILT UP YOUR CONFIDENCE WITH THE PROJECTS FOR USING SPICES DECORATIVELY IN THE HOME (SOME OF WHICH MAKE USEFUL GIFT ITEMS THEMSELVES), BUILD ON YOUR EXPERTISE TO MAKE UNUSUAL, IMAGINATIVE GIFTS FOR YOUR FAMILY AND FRIENDS. HERE'S A COUPLE OF GIFT IDEAS TO START YOU OFF: MASSAGE OIL IN SPICE-DECORATED BOTTLES AND TERRACOTTA POTS DECORATED WITH SPICES. THESE WOULD LOOK GREAT GIVEN AS A GIFT COMPLETE WITH PLANT.

Spicy Massage Oil

Spicy oil for use in massage or for adding to a bath makes a lovely gift, especially if presented in a bottle attractively decorated with spices.

The mixture of essential oils chosen here will give a sweet and spicy aroma, which is relaxing, uplifting, warming, and a tonic for the nervous system.

You Will Need

empty bottle

3 tbsp almond oil

16 drops lavender essential oil

10 drops juniper essential oil

2 drops ginger essential oil

2 drops cinnamon essential oil

star anise

gold powder

paintbrush

glue

1 Pour the carrier oil (almond oil is excellent) into a bowl. Mix in the essential oils, then pour into the bottle. Dip the star anise into the gold powder and glue onto the bottle in a row.

Alternatives

Try different shaped and colored bottles, and different spices, or ribbon. Tie with raffia, dried fruit or spices.

Peppercorn and Raffia Terracotta

Pots decorated with spices make an unusual and attractive alternative to plain pots. Terracotta pots, especially, with their warm color make a good background for the decorative spices, blending in well with their rich colors. In this example a plain pot and simple design are used, but you can try using more unusual shapes and more complicated patterns (see "Alternatives" below).

You Will Need

terracotta plant pot

black peppercorns

PVA or white glue

raffia

fine paintbrush

scissors

1 Tie a length of raffia around the top of the plant pot, choosing the length according to the look you wish to achieve. Tie a knot and snip off the ends.

2 Using the paintbrush, glue zigzags in fine lines and attach the peppercorns onto the zigzags. When the white glue dries, it becomes transparent.

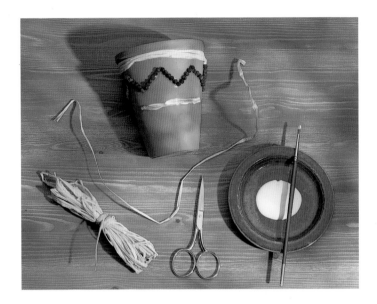

3 Paint a fine line of glue just beneath the zigzag peppercorns and tie another length of raffia around the pot. Cut and tie the ends carefully.

4 Make a neat, firm, bow out of a couple of lengths of raffia. Glue the back of the bow at the knot, then glue the bow onto the top of the pot.

Alternatives

Glue tiny chilies all around a plant pot in symmetrical rows.

Glue ribbon and raffia in vertical stripes around a vase and edge them with peppercorns.

SPICES FOR CHRISTMAS

SPICES CAN BE USED TO MAKE MANY WONDERFUL CHRISTMAS DECORATIONS, SUCH AS A CIRCLE TABLE DECORATION, SPICE BALLS, AND A KISSING WREATH.

Christmas Table Decoration

A circle table decoration is an attractive combination of spices and candles. The twelve night-lights represent the twelve days of Christmas, with the central church candle adding a dramatic touch. The heat of the candles will warm the spices, filling the room with a Christmasy aroma.

You Will Need

glass hors d'oeuvres bowl or lazy Susan

florists' oasis ring

(if you cannot find a ring, just cut out the shape you need)

12 night-lights

1 squat white candle

blue spruce fern or evergreen

blue spruce fern or evergreen

cloves

star anise

juniper berries

paprika powder

cinnamon sticks

black peppercorns

plastic tac or double-sided tape

cardboard

glue

1 ▷ Cut, fold, and tape cardboard into an upside-down T-shape, to act as a divider. The bottom should be wide enough to glue to the bowl. The height should be the same as the depth of the bowl. The length should be enough to reach between the central candle and the edge of the bowl. If you use an hors-d'oeuvres bowl, some of these sections may have already been made for you.

2 ▷ Glue 12 such dividers to the bottom of the bowl, so that they all meet at the central candle and separate the bowl into 12 even sections. Carefully fill each section with a different-colored spice, positioning a night-light at the center of each section. Place in the oasis ring and fill in with the blue spruce fern. Place a church candle in the center. Finally light all the candles and put in pride of place on your dining table. The spicy aromas will please the senses of your guests and make for a truly memorable meal.

Aromatic Christmas Wreath with Orange and Clove Pomanders

The use of orange and clove pomanders in this hanging wreath makes for a wonderfully aromatic traditional Christmas decoration. The fruit and spices blend perfectly.

You Will Need

a cane wreath

3 yards of red ribbon

holly or soft evergreens

three oranges

cloves

dish of Chinese mixed spices

florist's wire

1 Pierce the oranges with the cloves then dip them into a bowl of the mixed spices, cover and leave in a dark, cool space for a few days.

2 Take the cane circle and entwine the holly boughs around it, holding them in place with the florist's wire to cover it completely.

3 Wind the ribbon around the wreath, then attach lengths of ribbon at three equally divided points around the circle, to use in hanging.

4 From these points, attach more ribbon to hang down through the center of the wreath. Hang the orange pomanders from these.

Gift-Wrapped Box

This attractive box is very simple to make, and can be used to dress up any gift, for any occasion. It uses a few basic ingredients for stunning effect, and once you have the knack you can experiment to produce a great variety of gift boxes and packages (see "Alternatives" below).

1 Wrap the box with the ribbon. Start with the ribbon across the box, pass it under and cross over to right angles and then back over the top. Pass each end under the top ribbon, tie into a knot at the center.

You Will Need

one meter of bronze wired ribbon

oval-shaped wooden box

two dried apple slices

two dried orange slices

two cinnamon sticks

two dried cones

needle and thread

scissors

2 Sew the two apple slices together then sew onto ribbon at one side of knot.

3 Do the same with the dried orange slices, sewing them together then sewing them onto the other side of the knot.

5 Thread the cinnamon sticks through the bow at the center of the box, so that they cut diagonally through the cross formed by the bow.

4 Make a luxurious bow by tying the ends of the ribbon in a bow and then tying a second bow on top of that.

6 Finally attach the cones to the bow with a couple of tiny stitches, hiding them beneath the bow. Because they are so light they will be quite secure.

Alternatives

Wrap a square box with brown packaging paper, then glue a bundle of raffia onto the center top of the box. Add a couple of cinnamon sticks, cones and leaves, securing them in place with a tiny amount of glue.,
Thread tiny chilies and glass beads onto a length of cotton, string together with apple slices and bay leaves. Loop these onto the handle of a small brown paper bag.

THE SPICE DIRECTORY

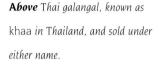

Above *Thai galangal, known as khaa in Thailand, and sold under either name.*

Below *Ground galangal, known as "Siamese ginger," or "Laos powder."*

GALANGAL
Alpinia galanga

AN ANCIENT ARABIC APHRODISIAC RECIPE SUGGESTS "MAKE A COMPOUND OF GALANGA, CUBEBS, SPARROW WORT, CARDAMOMS, NUTMEG, GILLY FLOWERS, INDIAN THISTLE, LAUREL SEEDS, CLOVES, AND PERSIAN PEPPER INTO A DRINK. TAKE TWICE DAILY MORNING AND NIGHT, IN PIGEON OR FOWL BROTH AND FOLLOWED BY WATER."

ORIGINS AND CHARACTERISTICS

Various spices come from the galangal family. Greater galangal comes from Southeast Asia. It has dark green, sword-like leaves on a reed-like stem. The flower consists of three petals with pink veins. The seed capsules are round and red in color. The root is an aromatic rhizome; the flesh is creamy white.

FLAVOR AND STORAGE

Greater galangal tastes of ginger and should be prepared as such. It is also available as a ground powder. Lesser galangal has an orangey-red color. When fresh, it is sliced or pounded to a pulp. It is also available in powdered form and as dried slices. Store slices and powder in an airtight container.

PROPERTIES

Culinary Galangal is now largely only used in Asian cooking, especially in curries and soups. While greater galangal can be used as a substitute for ginger, the lesser variety, although a member of the same family, must not be used in this way. The flowers and young shoots of the greater galangal are eaten raw, and the flowers of the lesser variety are often pickled. The lesser galangal is used in certain Asian dishes to give a pronounced aromatic flavor, as well as flavoring tea and the Russian liqueur Nastoika.

Kaempferia galangal (*Siphonochilus aethiopicus*) is another member of this family, the rhizome of which is used as a culinary spice in Ghana.

Medicinal Galangal is said to be good for digestive problems, ulcers, cholera, measles, and skin disorders, Kaempferia galangal for headaches, mouth abscesses, tetanus, coughs, and colds. The rhizome gives an essential oil used in perfumes, and in India for washing hair.

Lobster and Sweet Potato Curry

A luxury curry for a special occasion.

Serves 4–6

Preparation time 15 minutes. Cooking time about 20–25 minutes.

Ingredients

2 tbsp unsalted butter

1 lb sweet potatoes, peeled and cut into 1-inch cubes

1 tbsp sake or dry sherry

1 whole lobster, chopped into 1-inch cubes

Curry Sauce

1 tbsp vegetable oil

½ cup chopped onion

1 tbsp garlic, minced

2 tsp shrimp paste

1 dried chili, seeds removed, crushed

2 tsp cumin seeds

1 tbsp coriander seeds

1 tsp dried lemon grass, sliced

1 tsp ground galangal

2 tsp lemon rind, minced

2 tbsp chopped fresh coriander

1 tsp salt

1 tsp ground turmeric

2 tsp sweet paprika

Preparation

Make the curry sauce by heating the oil over medium-high heat. Add the onion and garlic and cook for 5 minutes or until soft. Add the shrimp paste and stir thoroughly, pressing the paste to blend it well. Cook for a further 3 or so minutes and remove from the heat.

Grind the chili, cumin seeds, coriander seeds, and lemon grass until powdery.

Place the onion mixture in a blender or food processor and blend until very smooth. Add the ground spices, galangal, lemon rind, fresh coriander, salt, turmeric, and paprika. Blend until the mixture becomes a smooth paste. This makes about ¼ cup curry sauce.

Melt the butter over medium heat and add the sweet potatoes. Cook for 15 minutes, taking care the potato does not burn. Stir in the curry sauce and sake together until the curry mixture is dissolved. Add the lobster cubes and cook for 2–3 more minutes.

Above Dill seed can be bought dry or fresh. **Opposite, top right** Dill weed is the leaves, chopped finely.

Below Dill, Anethum graveolens.

DILL
Anethum graveolens

DILL'S NAME COMES FROM THE OLD NORSE WORD DILLA, MEANING "LULL." THIS SPICE USED TO BE GIVEN IN A DECOCTION TO SOOTHE BABIES, AND IS STILL USED IN ENGLAND IN GRIPE WATER FOR COLIC. THE ENGLISH POET MICHAEL DRAYTON (1563–1630) MENTIONS DILL AS AN EXCELLENT INGREDIENT IN LOVE POTIONS.

ORIGINS AND CHARACTERISTICS

Dill is from the parsley family, and is native to the Mediterranean countries and southern Russia. It looks like a small fennel plant, growing to about 3 feet in height. The pale yellow flowers create pungent brown seeds, which are used as a spice. The seeds are collected as soon as the first few begin to drop. The heads are then cut off and dried in the sun. When completely dry, the seeds shake out easily from the head. The dark bluish-green, thread-like leaves are also rubbed from the dry stalk, chopped finely, and sold as "dillweed."

FLAVOR AND STORAGE

Dill tastes similar to caraway, and is often used as a milder alternative by those who find caraway too strong for their taste. It is also used as a substitute for fennel. Dill leaves have an aniseed flavor. The seeds have a slightly more bitter, sharp taste,and are easily crushed. Dill should be kept in a well-sealed container until needed.

PROPERTIES

Culinary Both the leaves and seeds of the dill plant are used in cooking, although the leaves do not have the same amount of oil as the seeds. The seeds are widely used in Scandinavian, German, and central and eastern European cooking. They combine well with cabbage, onions, all chutneys and relishes, root vegetables, bread, and pastries. It is delicious sprinkled over cottage or creamed cheese. The leaves are excellent with fish, rice, and egg dishes, and also make a very attractive garnish. Dill pickles are very popular.

This spice should be added during the last few minutes of cooking, as the flavor can soon be lost.

Medicinal Dill was used as a medicine 5,000 years ago by the ancient Egyptians, and continued to be popular in Europe up until the Middle Ages as a magic potion against witchcraft. It is reputedly a great help to digestion: when added to indigestible cucumbers, for instance, it will soothe the stomach. The Greeks use dill as a remedy for hiccups. A dill seed infusion is said to reduce stomach pains and cure insomnia. It is used in gripe water to soothe babies. Indian dill (*Anethum sowa*) has narrow, ridged seeds with an unusual flavor, which give an oil also used in the treatment of digestive pains.

Broiled Trout with Dill Sauce

These trout are broiled, but they can also be barbecued.

Serves 4

Preparation time 10 minutes, plus chilling. Cooking time 6–8 minutes.

Ingredients

4 trout (about 8 oz each), cleaned and boned

about 2 tbsp olive oil

salt, black pepper, paprika, for seasoning

Dill Sauce

5 tbsp sour cream

2 tbsp mayonnaise

1 tsp grated onion

1 tsp fresh lemon juice

2 tsp dried dillweed

1 tbsp dill seed, lightly toasted

Method

Combine all the sauce ingredients. Chill for several hours. **P**reheat the broiler. Lay the fish, skin side down, on a lightly greased broiler pan. Brush the fish with olive oil, then season. **P**lace the trout about 5 inches below the broiler. Cook until the flesh loses its translucency but is still juicy, 6–8 minutes. Remove from broiler and serve with the dill sauce.

CELERY SEED
Apium graveolens

THE ANCIENT GREEKS AND ROMANS USED CELERY SEEDS. UNTIL THE 17TH CENTURY THEY WERE TAKEN WITH COCOA AND KOLA NUTS AS A TONIC AND APHRODISIAC.

ORIGINS AND CHARACTERISTICS

Celery is part of the *umbelliferae* family, and grows in wet places throughout most of Europe, Asia, Africa, and South America. It is a perennial, with greenish flowers that produce seeds in their second year. Cultivated celery has swollen stalks mainly eaten raw in salads. Celeriac (*rapaceum*) is a variety in which the base of the stem becomes swollen, which is eaten as a vegetable. Celery seeds, the dried small, brownish fruit of the cultivated celery plant, are thought of as a western spice.

FLAVOR AND STORAGE

When ground, celery seeds become a type of salt. Commercial celery salt is salt with the addition of ground celery seeds or ground dried celery stems. It can be used instead of ordinary salt. Ground celery seeds should be stored in an airtight container.

PROPERTIES

Culinary Celery seed can be used as salt on salads and piquant dishes. It goes well with tomato juice, shrimp cocktails, white sauces, mayonnaise, cheese dishes, and tomato sauce for pasta. The seeds can be added to homemade bread, biscuits, pastries, and to butter.

Medicinal The distilled oil obtained from celery seeds can help detoxify the system. It is also said to reduce swelling, and so ease gout and arthritis. It is also antifungal and lightly sedative. The seeds are believed to be slightly toxic, so some people prefer them cooked, which also reduces their bitterness. For rheumatism, boil 1 oz celery seeds in 2½ cups water until the liquid is reduced by half, then strain, bottle, and cork. Take a teaspoonful twice a day.

Top Celery stalks are eaten raw in salads.

Above Celery, Apium graveolens.

Right Celery salt can be used instead of ordinary salt.

FRANKINCENSE AND MYRRH
Boswellia and Commiphora abyssinica

THE THREE WISE MEN BROUGHT THE INFANT JESUS GIFTS OF GOLD, FRANKINCENSE, AND MYRRH. LIKE GOLD, THESE TWO AROMATIC SPICES WERE HIGHLY VALUED BY THE ANCIENTS. THE GREEKS PRIZED A LIQUID FORM OF MYRRH CALLED STATE, AND FRANKINCENSE WAS USED IN CHINESE AND ARABIC MEDICINE.

Above *Frankincense resin is used as a healing essence.*

Left *Frankincense resin being collected from the Boswellia tree.*

ORIGINS AND CHARACTERISTICS

Their principal use is in incense and perfumery. They are both gums exuded from the barks of wild bushes, either naturally or from man-made cuts. The plants exude this sticky gum or resin as a protection when they are damaged. Frankincense gum is made from the milky liquid of a tree that grows wild in Africa and Asia. The gum hardens on contact with air, and turns a yellowy color.

Myrrh comes from a bush grown only in the basaltic soils of Somalia and Arabia. Its name is derived from the Hebrew word *mur*, meaning "bitter," as it has a bitter taste. It is a brownish-yellow liquid gum, which, as it hardens, turns into globules known as "tears." These are smaller than frankincense pieces, and are a mixture of colors, from light to dark orangey brown.

Above *Myrrh, Commiphora.*

Below *Myrrh, smaller than frankincense pieces.*

PROPERTIES

Medicinal and cosmetic Frankincense *Boswellia carteri* resin is used as a healing incense, often burned in a sacred setting. It is said to induce a meditative or contemplative state. Frankincense *Boswellia thurifera* is another source of resin distilled to produce oil used in rejuvenating skin creams.

Myrrh is also an ancient sacred incense, made from the oil of *Commiphora myrrha*. This is an anti-inflammatory and antiseptic oil, which was used for embalming. It is now used in toothpastes and perfume. Placing a little frankincense and myrrh in cupboards and drawers, or burning these spices on incense burners, will keep the air smelling beautifully sweet.

MUSTARD
Brassica nigra, Brassica alba

PREHISTORIC MAN IS KNOWN TO HAVE CHEWED MUSTARD SEEDS, AND THEY HAVE BEEN FOUND IN THE 1786 BC TOMB OF DIVA ABU'N-NEGE, NEAR THEBES IN ANCIENT EGYPT. IN THE 5TH CENTURY, THE CHINESE USED DRIED MUSTARD BURNT IN BALLS ON STOVES. THIS PRODUCED A TOXIC SMOKE WHICH THEY BELIEVED WOULD DRIVE AWAY THEIR ENEMIES—THE FIRST MUSTARD GAS.

Above Black mustard seeds are half the size of their white counterparts.

ORIGINS AND CHARACTERISTICS

Mustard is part of the *cruciferae* family, and is an easy plant to grow. It was naturally a biennial, but now annual strains have been cultivated. It has bright green oval leaves, four-petaled flowers that are yellow and grow in clusters in the summer, slender pods, and dark brown seeds that are crushed to make mustard paste. Mustard plants grow well in mountainous regions: not surprisingly, therefore, Nepal grows 79,000 tons a year, sending most of it to India. Russia, however, is also a major producer of mustard, using the oil from the seed for culinary purposes; Canada, too, is a major producer, exporting mainly to the United States. In the 18th century, the French city of Dijon, a name most people immediately associate with mustard, was making eighty different varieties of mustard paste; although they now make fewer types, they still supply over half the world's delicious spicy mustard condiments.

Brassica alba is a white or yellow mustard. *Brassica nigra* is a black seed, half the size of the white seed, probably introduced to Europe by early Arab traders. Today it is only grown where there is plentiful cheap labor, because the seed has to be gathered very carefully by hand. The seeds are so tiny that when the plant is shaken they fall off and are lost. *Brassica juncea* is a brown seed from an Indian mustard that grows 4–6 feet high. It is picked by huge machines that can scoop up millions of seeds in one go.

Below Black mustard, Brassica nigra, *is an easy plant to grow. The four-petaled flowers are bright yellow.*

FLAVOR AND STORAGE

Mustard seeds have a very earthy, sweet taste. Before the discovery of chilies, it was very popular for its pungency. Mustard is used in flower and seed form, while the latter can be ground into powder and used in pastes

Mustard oil can also be bought in ethnic Indian grocery stores, if you can find these, but it can go rancid quickly and needs to be stored in a corked bottle in a cool place. It is maybe better—and easier—to fry seeds in hot oil (they pop in much the same way as dried corn kernels) to make your own flavored oil.

Ground mustard powder must be mixed with cold water to activate the enzymes needed to release the pungency. Putting it in boiling water kills the enzymes, and vinegar inhibits them, both creating a weak aroma and bitter taste. Fresh seeds can be ground in a coffee grinder. If a recipe asks for lightly ground seeds, be careful not to turn them into a powder, but leave them in halves or quarters. The seeds are best kept in an airtight jar. The powder is safe kept in the cardboard in the carton or can that it is bought in. Old mustard seeds tend to become a little bitter, but they can still be used as a seasoning.

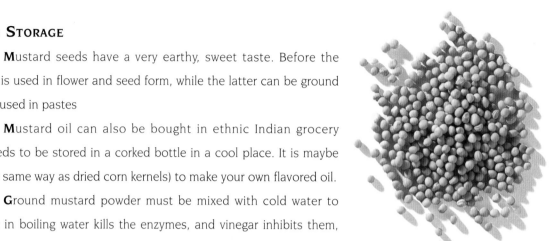

Above Brassica alba *is white or yellow mustard. Yellow mustard seeds are much larger than brown or black.*

PROPERTIES

Culinary Mustard combines easily with other flavors, making it a very popular addition to dishes such as vegetable curries, pastries, and toppings to cheese crackers. In Indian cuisine, seeds are fried as a garnish for *dhal*. It is most common as a table condiment, often mixed with horseradish. Black mustard seed has the strongest flavor, but, as it is so difficult to harvest, brown mustard seeds are more commonly used. The seeds are used for pickling, and can be put whole into very hot oil and popped. Raw foods can then be cooked in this flavored oil, or it can be poured over some dishes just before serving. The flowers make a pretty addition to salads.

Many nationalities enjoy their own forms of mustard. English mustard, a blend of white and brown seeds, is yellow and very hot, with turmeric added for vibrancy. American mustard is yellow, but much milder. German mustard is smooth, hot, and horseradishy. Italians go for mustard-flavored fruit relishes, especially mustard mixed with grapes. The Japanese enjoy brown mustard seeds, served as a very hot mustard dip with raw fish. The French still favor the Dijon mustard, while Russians use the oil more than the mustard itself.

Below *Brown mustard seeds. English mustard is a blend of white and brown.*

Medicinal Mustard plasters or poultices were used regularly to stimulate the blood. Applied to the painful areas for 10 minutes, they would increase blood circulation, causing some redness on the skin. If left too long or applied too strong, the skin could blister. White mustard was said to be a great cleanser of the alimentary system, as an emetic and laxative. The crushed seeds were drunk soaked in a hot, sweet solution. The Romans mixed mustard with oil to make a massage oil to ease stiff muscles. A strong infusion of mustard seed was believed to be an erotic stimulant, and hot mustard baths have been recommended to arouse women's libido.

Above *English yellow mustard seeds.*

An old Irish remedy for asthma called for mustard and garlic to be added to white wine and left for a week, then drunk in quantity. For clear voices, it was recommended that dried mustard powder was mixed into little balls with honey; two or three swallowed every morning was promised to have singers sounding like angels. The English herbalist Nicholas Culpeper, in his H*erbal* (1653), recommends mustard and honey for coughs. A pinch of mustard in cold water is a remedy for hiccups. Mustard baths were popular for practically everything. Mustard ointment or a mustard footbath was believed extremely good for chilblains. Today mustard is only used by homeopaths, who use the black seed for nose, ear, and throat problems.

Herb, Garlic, and Mustard Dressing

This is a quite strongly flavored dressing.

makes about 1 *cup*

Preparation time 10 minutes.

Ingredients

1–2 garlic cloves

leaves from 4–5 sprigs of thyme

leaves and fine stems from a small bunch of chervil

1 tsp Dijon mustard

¼ cup red wine vinegar

¾ cup olive oil

Preparation

Put the garlic, herbs, and a pinch of salt into a bowl. Crush together, then stir in the vinegar and mustard until smooth. **S**lowly pour in the oil, whisking constantly, until well emulsified. Season with pepper.

CAPER

Capparis spinosa

PICKLED CAPERS HAVE BEEN USED AS A CONDIMENT IN SOUTHERN EUROPE FOR OVER 2,000 YEARS.

Below The flowers of the Caper plant, Capparis spinosa, *are short-lived, with white petals streaked with pale pink and purple stamens.*

ORIGINS AND CHARACTERISTICS

Caper is a minor spice that is the small, wrinkled, sun-dried bud of a trailing shrub from the Mediterranean, which grows wild and is regarded as a weed. It has thick, shiny leaves, and short-lived flowers with white petals streaked with pale pink and purple stamens.

FLAVOR AND STORAGE

This spice has a very sharp taste, and needs to be used in moderation. The flavor develops when the capers are pickled in vinegar. They are sold in jars of vinegar or salted water to help preserve them.

PROPERTIES

Culinary Capers are widely used in North African dishes, and are especially popular in Sardinia, where you will find them added to *caponata*, a salad of eggplant and tuna. They can also be added to spicy dishes, sauces such as tartar, or used as a garnish for hors d'oeuvres.

Capers are an excellent accompaniment to oily fish and salty food such as salted meat or fish. Pickled broombuds (*genista*) can be used as a substitute for capers.

Medicinal Capers reputedly increase appetite and aid digestion. They help gastrointestinal infections and diarrhea, and can be taken as an infusion for coughs.

Right *Capers are widely used in*
North African dishes.

Cauliflower and Celery Stir Fry

A vegetarian stir fry with a sweet sour dressing.

serves 4–6

Preparation time 10 minutes. Cooking time 25 minutes.

Ingredients

3 tbsp oil

1 small onion, halved and thinly sliced

½ small cauliflower, broken into small flowerets

1 celery heart, thinly sliced

salt and freshly ground black pepper

½ cup black olives, sliced

1 sweet eating apple, cored and roughly chopped

1 tbsp capers, chopped

1 tbsp soft brown sugar

1–2 tbsp cider vinegar

Preparation

Heat the oil and stir fry the onion for 5 minutes before adding the cauliflower and celery. Stir fry the vegetables until they are lightly cooked—they should not taste raw but should still be crunchy. This takes about 15 minutes, depending on the heat and the size of the pan.

Add seasoning, the olives, apple, and capers, and continue to stir fry for 2 minutes. Make a well in the middle of the vegetables and add the sugar and 1 tbsp of the vinegar. Stir the juices until the sugar dissolves, then toss the small amount of dressing with the vegetables. Taste and add the remaining vinegar if liked. Serve at once.

PAPRIKA
Capsicum annuum

RESEARCHERS IN THE UNITED STATES HAVE ATTEMPTED TO EXPLAIN WHY HOT SPICES LIKE PAPRIKA ARE PLEASANT TO TASTE. IT SEEMS THE BURNING SENSATION IS THE PAIN OF NERVE ENDINGS ON THE TONGUE. THIS RELEASES ENDORPHINS, THE BODY'S NATURAL PAINKILLERS, GIVING RISE TO PLEASURABLE AND EVEN EUPHORIC SENSATIONS.

Below *Sweet peppers are the fruit of* Capsicum annuum.

ORIGINS AND CHARACTERISTICS

Paprika powder is ground from dried sweet peppers, the fruits of a tropical evergreen bush that grows to about 3 feet. It is indigenous to Central America, but is now cultivated in Spain, Turkey, Hungary, and the United States. It is not actually a pepper, but is of the *solanceae* family and a relative of chili. Cultivation of this pepper in the northern hemisphere has eliminated the capsaicin content that provides the heat in chilies, so paprika is milder. It is also made from peppers that have been dried with their hot seeds removed first. The best paprika is rich, bright red, and made with peppers from Hungary, which is why Hungarian goulash is so famous.

FLAVOR AND STORAGE

In Western Europe and the United States, paprika has a distinctive russet color and a mild, sweet flavor with a cardamom aroma. In Hungary, it also comes in a highly aromatic and hot variety, which is lighter in color. Spanish paprika is the hottest. Although paprika is used in larger amounts than many spices, it is best to buy it in small quantities since it loses its aroma and flavor quickly. Store in an airtight container away from sunlight.

Above *Paprika is ground from dried sweet peppers.*

PROPERTIES

Culinary Paprika is a highly versatile spice. It is good with eggs, fish, chicken, crab and cheese. It can also be used on baked potatoes, salads, rice dishes, and tomatoes and sour cream.

Medicinal Paprika is rich in vitamin C, and so helps colds and influenza. It is also said to treat digestive troubles, cramps, circulation problems, and shingles.

Hungarian Herring Salad

Some of the most wonderful herring dishes come from Hungary, where fish has been pickled for centuries.

serves 4–6

Preparation time 15 minutes, plus standing.

Ingredients

2 pickled herrings

3 hard-cooked eggs

2 medium boiled potatoes

2 red apples, cored and seeded

1 tbsp chopped onion

¼ cup vinegar

¼ cup olive oil

½ tsp prepared mustard

salt

mild and sweet paprika

Preparation

Slice herring into small pieces and place in a serving dish. Dice eggs, potatoes, and apples. Add to the dish with the onion. **B**lend the vinegar, oil, and mustard together, and season to taste with the salt and paprika. Pour over the salad, and toss gently to coat. Leave to stand for 30 minutes before serving, then sprinkle with paprika to add a dash of color.

CHILI PEPPERS
Capsicum frutescens

A NATIVE OF PERU, CHILI PEPPER WAS WIDELY CULTIVATED IN CENTRAL AND SOUTH AMERICA BEFORE THE EUROPEANS ARRIVED. THE AZTECS USED IT TO FLAVOR THEIR COCOA. SOMEWHAT LESS COSILY, THEY ALSO USED TO PUNISH THEIR CHILDREN BY HOLDING THEM OVER BURNING CHILIES, AND IF A YOUNG GIRL GAZED TOO LONG AT A HANDSOME MAN, SHE HAD CHILI RUBBED INTO HER EYES.

Ripe red chili peppers

ORIGINS AND CHARACTERISTICS

Chilies are the fruits of the pungent types of capsicums. They are native to Central and South America, but are now grown in many tropical and subtropical areas. They were brought to the West by explorers of the New World who had set out in search of pepper. These elongated, long, thin pods were called red peppers first by these Spanish explorers, because of their color and hot taste. The Spaniards were amazed how the natives of Mexico and Peru could eat chilies like they themselves ate fruit. Mexicans still hardly ever eat without first flavoring their meal with this fiery spice.

In fact, chilies are not a relation of the black peppercorn, but belong to the *Solanacae* family, which also includes deadly nightshade, eggplant, tomatoes, potatoes, sweet bell peppers, and tobacco. Around 200 varieties of chili are known to be grown in the tropics, as well as many local varieties that have not been documented. They contain capsaicin, which gives them their heat. This is measured in units called Scovilles, and, depending on the variety, varies from 0 to 300,000—mild to scorchingly hot.

Above *Chili peppers*, Capsicum frutescens, *growing.*
Below *Unripe chili peppers.*

FLAVOR AND STORAGE

There is a wide variety of chilies available. They can be bought whole, both dried and fresh. When they are ripe they are yellow and red, while the unripe chili is green. The green ones are the hottest, the seeds being the hottest part. Fresh peppers should be smooth and unwrinkled. Authentic chili powder is the commercial flavoring used in the hottest chilies, as opposed to Mexican chili powder, which is much milder, due to other ingredients that are added to tone down the fierceness. The finely ground cayenne powder is a blend of various types of dried chilies. Chili powder is also available in a Texan-style blend of chilies, cumin, oregano, and garlic.

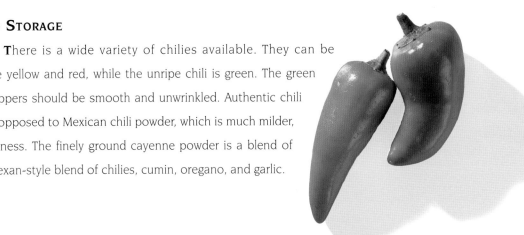

Above Right Chilies are available in a wide variety. The green ones are the hottest.

Above Dried, crushed chilies.

Below Dried Bird's eye chilies.

Fresh peppers will keep for a short time in the salad section of a refrigerator, but need to be eaten as soon as possible. The powder is best stored in screwtop jars kept in a dry, dark place. Chili oil is a red, transparent liquid bought in bottles, and can be kept for long periods. It is very hot, and should be used sparingly. It can be a substitute of Tabasco sauce or chili sauce.

PROPERTIES

Culinary These spices are used to give a hot peppery flavor to many foods, and are widely used in Mexican and Southeast Asian cookery. In the 16th century, the Portuguese introduced chilies to their Indian colonies and they have been indispensable to Indian cuisine ever since. The hot vindaloo curries are made from the hottest chilies. The very hot bird's eye peppers are used mainly in relishes; they are very powerful, and should be treated with extreme caution. Mexican chili powder is used in Mexican guacamole, salsas, chili con carne, Boston baked beans, and deviled eggs. Tabasco sauce is a blend of hot chilies and vinegar. Cayenne pepper is an ingredient in Newburg sauce.

The longer chilies are cooked, the hotter the dish will become. It is best to use a whole chili so you can remove it at the end of cooking. The greatest heat is in the seeds, so if you find the taste too strong, remove the seeds by slicing the pepper lengthwise and easing them out with a pointed utensil. If you burn your mouth by adding too much chili to a dish, take milk or cold beer to reduce the burning—water will not help!

Medicinal Chilies are said to help cramps, circulation problems, and paralysis, as well as easing shingles. They have a high vitamin C content, and so are good for colds and influenza. They are an ingredient in certain gargles, and the infused oil can be used to give a warming massage to relieve rheumatism. They are also recommended for treating digestive troubles, although eating too many can also burn the mouth and stomach.

Hot peppers should be handled with care, so always wash your hands after handling them. If you do not, touching a sensitive area of skin or the eyes can lead to painful burning. Perhaps this is why some Shamans carry peppers in the belief that they have the power to ward off ghouls, ghosts, and other evil spirits.

AJOWAN
Carum ajowan

AJOWAN IS ALSO KNOWN AS AJWAIN AND BISHOP'S WEED. IT IS NOT A POPULAR SPICE, AND FOR THIS REASON IS OFTEN ONLY AVAILABLE IN ETHNIC INDIAN STORES, WHICH ARE OFTEN THEMSELVES VERY HARD TO FIND.

ORIGINS AND CHARACTERISTICS

Ajowan is part of the *umbelliferae* family, to which parsley and cumin also belong. It is native to southern India, but is now more widespread and also grown in Egypt, Iran, Pakistan, and Afghanistan.

Dried ajowan seed

FLAVOR AND STORAGE

The seeds that form the spice have a strong, pungent flavor similar to pepper and anise. They contain thymol oil, which gives a taste reminiscent of thyme, for which it can also be a convincing substitute. Store in an airtight container.

PROPERTIES

Culinary Ajowan is practically confined to Indian cookery alone. It is used in Indian lentil dishes with oregano and black pepper, vegetable *parathas* (a flat bread) and meat dishes. It is added sparingly to beans, pulses, pakoras, tangy biscuits, and Indian breads.

CARAWAY
Carum carvi

CARAWAY SEEDS HAVE BEEN EATEN SINCE STONE AGE TIMES. THE ANCIENT EGYPTIANS, WHO PLACED THIS SPICE WITH THEIR DEAD TO KEEP BAD SPIRITS AWAY, MENTIONED IT IN A PAPYRUS DATED AS EARLY AS 2500 BC. HERE IN THE UNITED STATES, IT WAS GIVEN TO CHILDREN IN CHURCH TO HELP THEM STOP FIDGETING, AND SO EARNED THE NICKNAME "MEETIN' SEED." IT IS SAID THAT IF TAME PIGEONS ARE FED CARAWAY BREAD THEY ARE LESS LIKELY TO STRAY. IN FOLKLORE, CARAWAY IS THOUGHT TO PREVENT FICKLENESS, AND IS A COMMON INGREDIENT OF LOVE POTIONS. IT IS ALSO FREQUENTLY CLAIMED TO BE AN APHRODISIAC IN ORIENTAL LOVE MANUALS.

ORIGINS AND CHARACTERISTICS

Caraway is from the *umbelliferae* family. It is native to Europe and Western Asia. It grows wild, but is now commercially cultivated. The plant is a biennial that grows to 2 feet in height, with fine, feathery leaves, and umbels of small white, sometimes pink, flowerheads. It produces capsules containing two curved, narrow seeds, which explode when ripe to release the seeds. The thick, tapering root is an aromatic vegetable.

FLAVOR AND STORAGE

The seeds that form the spice are long and thin, with a tangy, somewhat sharp taste. They can be used whole or ground, and should be stored in airtight containers in a cool place. If the seeds are used whole, they should be added at the end of cooking to prevent the flavor turning bitter.

PROPERTIES

Culinary Caraway is used to decorate bread, biscuits, crackers, cakes, and is added to dumplings, rye bread, and muffins. It can be sprinkled onto cooked cabbage or put in cheese dips for appetizers, makes a tasty addition to most soups, fish, meat, salads, cheese flans, and is used in pickling. The essential oil is an important ingredient in the liqueur kümmel, as well as flavoring confectionery and gin.

Below *Caraway,* Carum carvi, *is a member of the parsley family.*

Medicinal Caraway seeds are eaten raw or sugar-coated as comfits after a meal to prevent gas and to sweeten the breath. Caraway aids digestion, is good for babies with colic, and helps nursing mothers to promote milk secretion. It is also used in mouthwashes, perfumes, and aftershaves. Applied externally, a poultice of caraway seeds is good for ear infections. In India, it is used in soaps, and it was recommended that pale-faced maidens rub it into their skins to tone their complexion.

Pork with Sauerkraut

Simple, yet full of flavor, serve this stir fry with boiled or baked potatoes or cooked buckwheat.

Serves 4

Preparation time 10 minutes, plus marinating.
Cooking time about 25 minutes.

Ingredients

1 lb lean boneless pork, diced
1 tsp paprika
1 garlic clove, crushed
1 tbsp caraway seeds
salt and freshly ground black pepper
3 tbsp oil
1 onion, chopped
1 bay leaf
1 large sage sprig
2 full-flavored eating apples, peeled, cored and diced
1 lb sauerkraut, well drained and shredded
½ cup sour cream or thick yogurt

Preparation

Mix the pork, paprika, garlic, caraway (if used), and seasoning so that all the meat is well coated in the flavoring ingredients. The meat benefits from being left to marinate for a few hours (or overnight in the refrigerator), but this is not essential. Heat the oil, then stir fry the onion, bay leaf, and sage for 3 minutes. Add the pork with all the seasoning and stir fry over fairly high heat for 5 minutes. Add the apples, then continue to stir fry until the pork is well cooked. Add the sauerkraut and stir fry for a few minutes to heat the vegetable through.

When the sauerkraut is piping hot, stir in the sour cream or yogurt to moisten the mixture. Taste and adjust the seasoning and stir for a few seconds, but do not overcook as the cream or yogurt will curdle.

Caraway seed

CASSIA
Cinnamomum cassia

Cassia bark

CASSIA WAS ONE OF VARIOUS SPICES USED BY ANCIENT EGYPTIANS TO EMBALM THEIR PHARAOHS AND NOBLES. IN ANCIENT ARABIA, IT WAS USED IN SACRED RITUALS, OFFERINGS TO THE SUN, AND TO LIGHT THE SACRED ALTAR FIRES WHEN SACRIFICES WERE MADE. IN INDONESIA, A BRIDE IS TRADITIONALLY GIVEN A PAIR OF CASSIA BUDS THAT HAVE BEEN GROWING SIDE BY SIDE ON THE TREE, AS A GOOD-LUCK TOKEN.

ORIGINS AND CHARACTERISTICS

Cassia is made from the aromatic bark of an evergreen plant of the laurel family, which has tiny cream flowers and purple berries. It is used and sold simply as "cinnamon" in the United States. The bark, which is thicker than cinnamon, is harvested during the rainy season. The shoots are peeled, then rubbed to loosen the inner bark, which is split and removed. The peels are then telescoped into one another, forming a quill, and then filled with trimmings of the same quality to maintain the cylindrical shape. The bark is dried in the sun for a few days, then rolled and placed in more subdued sunlight, where it continues drying. Finally, it is bleached and graded, ready for sale.

Cassia originates in China. Today, it is also grown elsewhere, particularly Indonesia and India. It is known as Chinese cinnamon, and was used in China over 2,500 years ago, when it was more precious than gold. The name of the river Kwei means "cassia," and the name of the Chinese province Kweilin translates as "cassia forest." The spice that originally traveled to the West on the "cinnamon route" was actually cassia, not cinnamon.

FLAVOR AND STORAGE

Cassia is very similar to cinnamon in both flavor and appearance. Cassia can soon lose much of its flavor, and both sticks and ground forms must be kept in airtight jars.

PROPERTIES

Culinary Cassia is one of the five spices in Chinese five-spice mixture. It is an essential ingredient in a traditional Chinese fish sauce, with soy sauce, rice wine, and broth. It is also used in chocolate and liqueurs, and is sometimes stirred into coffee or rum to add flavor. Cassia is excellent in all tangy dishes, especially curries, pilau rice, and Chinese recipes.

CINNAMON

Cinnamomum verum, C. loureirii, C. zeylanicum

CINNAMON IS THE OLDEST SPICE TO HAVE BEEN TRADED, BEING RECORDED AS FAR BACK AS 2500 BC. IN 500 BC, HIPPOCRATES WROTE OF ITS IMPORTANT MEDICINAL PROPERTIES. IT WAS PROBABLY BROUGHT TO THE MIDDLE EAST BY PHOENICIAN TRADERS, AND, IN OLD TESTAMENT TIMES, IT WAS USED AS A PERFUME AND AS AN INGREDIENT IN THE ANOINTING OIL USED BY MOSES IN THE TABERNACLE. IT HAS BEEN USED IN EUROPE SINCE THE 9TH CENTURY.

Below Cinnamon, Cinnamomum zeylanicum, *grows very tall.*

ORIGINS AND CHARACTERISTICS

Cinnamon comes from the dried inner bark of certain tropical/Asian trees in the genus Cinnamomum, especially C. *verum* and C. *loureirii*. In Britain, however, only the Sri Lankan bark known as *Cinnamomum zeylanicum* can be called cinnamon—the rest are cassia. The best cinnamon grows within sight of the sea, in subtropical conditions. The tree grows very tall, with long, deeply veined leaves that are dark green above and lighter below. The flowers are small and yellow, the berries dark and purple. It is the bark that is used in cooking.

Cinnamon is propagated by cuttings or by seed planted in groups of four and five. Germination takes about three weeks. Every two or three years the shoots are cut back to the ground; the bark is then peeled off the cut shoots and left for a day. The outer bark is then stripped off, and, as the inner bark dries, it rolls up into light brown quills, about an inch in diameter. While still damp, smaller quills are inserted into the larger ones, and, as they dry out, they become tightly coiled together.

FLAVOR AND STORAGE

Cinnamon is a sweet-tasting spice, with a warm, woody aroma. The thinnest bark is the best-quality cinnamon, and has the finest fragrance and taste. Cinnamon can be bought as sticks or ground. When ground, the flavor becomes stronger, but because it quickly loses its aroma, this spice must always be stored in an airtight jar and should be discarded if kept for several months. Broken sticks are called quillings and have a less powerful aroma, but are useful for imparting flavor in slow cooking. Whatever use you have in mind, it is best to buy whole sticks and crush them yourself, if desired, in a mortar and pestle.

PROPERTIES

Culinary Whole cinnamon sticks are used for spicing hot drinks, especially mulled wine and punch. They can also be used in fruit punches and with fresh or stewed fruits. In Mexico, cinnamon is used in chocolate, and Mexicans often stir hot chocolate drinks with

Ground cinnamon

cinnamon sticks. Ground cinnamon is a frequent addition to breads and cakes, and to a wealth of sweet dishes, imparting a delicious, warm, spicy flavor to fruit pies— especially apple. It can also be used in more piquant dishes, such as curries, and combines perfectly with chicken.

Medicinal Cinnamon is said to be a strong stimulant for the glandular system, and helpful for stomach upsets. It is also good for colds and sore throats. In the past, cinnamon was used as a breath freshener and as a tonic for the whole system, as well as being given as a sedative to mothers during childbirth. In Sri Lanka, it is one of the ingredients of a spiced tea given to visitors at the Government Spice Gardens, which is said to have cured many ailments.

Cinnamon sticks

Cinnamon Diamond Cookies

These refrigerator cookies are sweet and crisp—
just the thing to serve with ice cream.

Makes about 60

Preparation time 20 minutes, plus chilling.

Cooking time 10 minutes per batch.

Ingredients

2¼ cups all-purpose flour

½ tsp salt

1 tbsp ground cinnamon

1 cup (2 sticks) unsalted butter, softened

¾ cup packed light-brown sugar

2 eggs, lightly beaten

1 tsp vanilla extract

½ cup superfine sugar for sprinkling

1 tsp ground cinnamon

1 egg yolk beaten with 2 tbsp water for glazing

Preparation

Into a medium bowl, sift together the flour, salt, and 1 tablespoon cinnamon.

In a large bowl with electric mixer, beat the butter until creamy, 30 seconds. Add the brown sugar and continue beating until light and fluffy, 1–2 minutes. Gradually beat in the eggs and vanilla extract until well blended. Stir in the flour mixture.

Divide the dough in half, and scrape onto a piece of plastic wrap or waxed paper. Using the wrap or paper as a guide, form each dough half into a log about 2 inches in diameter; flatten the log on 4 sides to form a rectangular shape. Wrap tightly, and refrigerate several hours or overnight until firm. (Dough can be made ahead up to 5 days or frozen.)

Lightly grease 2 large baking sheets. In a small bowl, combine the superfine sugar and 1 tsp cinnamon. With a sharp knife, cut the log into ¼-inch squares and place 1 inch apart on the prepared baking sheets. Brush each square with a little egg yolk; then, using a sharp knife, score each to make a diamond pattern, and sprinkle with a little sugar-cinnamon mixture.

Bake at 375°F. until golden, about 10 minutes. Remove the baking sheets to wire racks to cool slightly. Then, using a metal pancake turner or palette knife, remove the cookies to wire racks to cool completely. Repeat with the remaining cookie dough and sugar mixture. Store in airtight containers.

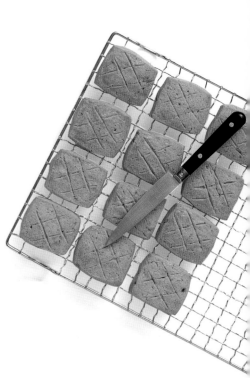

CITRUS
Citrus hystrix, C. Bergamia, etc.

THE CITRUS GENUS INCLUDES ABOUT 16 SPECIES OF EVERGREEN TREES AND SHRUBS, WITH SCENTED FLOWERS AND SEGMENTED FRUITS. THE THIN, SMOOTH PEEL OF CITRUS BERGAMIA YIELDS SWEETSMELLING BERGAMOT OIL, WHICH IS USED IN GENUINE EAU DE COLOGNE, PERFUMES, COSMETICS, AND MOST FAMOUSLY TO FLAVOR EARL GREY TEA. PERFUMES WITH BERGAMOT SHOULD NEVER BE WORN ON THE SKIN IN THE SUN, HOWEVER, AS IT INCREASES PHOTOSENSITIVITY AND CAN BE DANGEROUS. CITRUS HYSTRIX (KAFFIR LIME) HAS AROMATIC LEAVES THAT ARE ESPECIALLY POPULAR IN THAI AND INDONESIAN COOKING.

ORIGINS AND CHARACTERISTICS

Below *Kaffir lime,* Citrus hystrix, *growing in Costa Rica.*

Citrus grow in well-drained, moist soil in Southeast Asia and the Pacific Islands. *Citrus aurantium* is a bitter orange produced by a tree with leathery leaves that grows about 33 feet high. *Citrus bergamia* has highly scented white flowers and aromatic fruit, with oval, pointed leaves. *Citrus reticulata* is a small tree with fragrant white flowers, and dark green glossy leaves; the fruits are small mandarins, with thin skins, which turn from green to yellow to deep orange when ripe. *Citrus aurantifolia* is a tree bearing pointed leaves with short, sharp spines in the leaf axils. It has small, white flowers and the greeny-yellow fruit known as limes. Kaffir lime is a small tree with double leaves and a pear-shaped, wrinkly, warty, green fruit. It is the fresh or dried leaves, juice,and grated peel of the Kaffir lime that have culinary uses.

FLAVOR AND STORAGE

These spices are very bitter. Kaffir is a variety of lime that is inedible, the fruit being very dry and sour. Kaffir lime leaves are usually sold dried, and should always be soaked before use. Do not use the water that you have used for soaking because this is very bitter, and must be discarded. If Kaffir lime leaves are unavailable, fresh citrus leaves can be substituted. The rind can be bought dried in strips, in specialized Asian shops where it is known as *makrut*. Whole limes can be frozen for later use, and the dried leaves can be stored in a glass jar. Make sure it is airtight.

Dried Kaffir lime leaves

PROPERTIES

Culinary The fruit, juice, and peel of citrus fruits are used to flavor food and drinks. *Citrus aurantifolia* is popular in tropical cookery. Kaffir lime leaves are very aromatic and are used especially in Thai and Indonesian cooking, as is the grated rind. The leaves give a wonderful flavor to Thai shrimp soup.

Medicinal and cosmetic The fruit, juice, and peel of citrus fruits contain vitamin C, which is good for building up a resistance to coughs and colds. The juice is antiseptic and astringent, and will also lighten hair. The essential oil from the peel is a stimulant and helps purify water, as well as being used to scent food, cosmetics, and perfume.

The flowers, shoots, and seeds of *citrus aurantium* all yield essential oils, and a by-product is orange-flower water. The bitter orange flowers of *citrus aurantium* supply neroli oil for perfumes and aromatherapy, while the leaves and young shoots give the lighter petit-grain oil, which treats depression and anxiety. *Citrus bergamia* is good for depression, skin disorders, and urinary problems. The rind of *citrus reticulata* is used in Chinese medicine for chest complaints, congestion, and malaria.

CORIANDER
Coriandrum sativum

CORIANDER HAS BEEN A POPULAR SPICE SINCE ANCIENT TIMES, AND IS MENTIONED IN EARLY EGYPTIAN, SANSKRIT, AND GREEK TEXTS. THE GREEKS USED IT TO FLAVOR WINE, WHILE IT WAS VALUED AS AN APHRODISIAC BY THE EGYPTIANS. THE 13TH-CENTURY OCCULTIST AND PHILOSOPHER, ALBERTUS MAGNUS, ALSO STATES THAT, WHEN GATHERED IN THE LAST QUARTER OF THE MOON, CORIANDER IS A "LOVE-PRODUCING HERB."

ORIGINS AND CHARACTERISTICS

Coriander is a member of the parsley family. It is native to southern Europe and the East, but is now grown in many parts of the world. An annual plant, it grows to 2 feet in height, with dainty flowers that have a pinky-mauve tinge. The seeds used as a spice are round to oval in shape, and turn from bright green to beige as they ripen. Interestingly, coriander's name comes from the Greek *koris*, meaning "bug." It acquired this title because the unripe coriander seeds have a rather unpleasant odor, which is similar to that given off by a certain type of green beetle. The ripe seeds, however, are delightfully fragrant.

FLAVOR AND STORAGE

This spice tastes sweet and tangy, with a slightly citrus flavor. In India, they gently roast the seeds before use. Although not hot, its mild, slightly bitter taste is a necessary ingredient of many curry and other spice mixes. Coriander is usually sold in a powdered form, although the whole, dried seeds are available.

The leaves, which are an herb, have a different taste and are used fresh. They have an orangey, pungent flavor and resemble parsley, for which they are often substituted; this explains the plant's colloquial name, "Chinese parsley." The leaves do not stay fresh for many days, and need to be used immediately. The seeds and powder must be kept in an airtight container.

Coriander seed

PROPERTIES

Culinary Coriander seeds taste excellent in practically everything. Because they aid digestion, they are particularly effective with carbohydrates like pastries and bread. The root and stem can be added to beans when being cooked, to improve the smell and reduce the side effects that cause flatulence. A little coriander powder can be sprinkled over fish and savory dishes as a healthy alternative to salt. It is also popular in relishes and ratatouilles, as well as to flavor liqueurs. Ground coriander is great on baked apples and other baked fruits.

In India, the powder is a basic ingredient of curry powder, and the fresh root is often used as well. In France, cooking this spice forms the basis of vegetable dishes *à la grecque*. Eastern and Mediterranean cooking use coriander leaves as a garnish, in soups, and in curries. The seeds are excellent added to vodka and left to infuse for a couple of days.

Medicinal The spicy essential oil distilled from coriander seeds is used to flavor unpleasant medicines, as an ingredient for toothpaste, and in perfumes and incense. Added to massage oil, it is particularly good for facial neuralgia and cramps. It is renowned as an aid to digestion; and the seeds are mild sedatives and ease migraines. If animals eat coriander in large quantities, it has a narcotic effect: its nickname is "dizzycorn."

Ground coriander

Dried coriander leaf

Coriander Potatoes

Coriander works wonders for new potatoes, complementing their sweet fresh flavor perfectly.

serves 4

Preparation time 10 minutes, plus marinating.

Cooking time 30 minutes.

Ingredients

2 lb small new potatoes, scrubbed and boiled

salt and freshly ground black pepper

2 tsp superfine sugar

2 tbsp lemon juice

4 tbsp olive oil

3 tbsp crushed coriander seeds

strip of lemon

4 tbsp snipped chives

Preparation

Cook the potatoes in boiling, slightly salted water for 10–15 minutes, or until tender. Drain. Stir the sugar and lemon juice together until the sugar dissolves.

Heat the oil and stir fry the coriander for 2 minutes.

Add the lemon rind and continue to cook for a further minute, pressing the piece of rind to bring out its flavor. Tip the potatoes into the pan and then stir fry them for about 10 minutes, or until they are just beginning to brown on the outside.

Pour the sweetened lemon juice over the potatoes and mix them well with the oil in the pan, so that the liquids mingle to form a hot dressing. Mix in the chives, check the seasoning, and serve at once.

SAFFRON
Crocus sativus

The name saffron comes from the Arabic Za'faran, meaning "yellow." The praises of this spice are sung in the biblical Song of Solomon. The ancient Greeks clothed their gods and goddesses in saffron-colored robes, and Roman ladies used it to dye their hair golden. In India, it is regarded as a sacred dye, and the people wear a saffron paste mark on the forehead called a tillak. Shortly after the Buddha's death, his devotees made saffron the official color of their robes, which it still is. The English herbalist Nicholas Culpeper called saffron "a herb of the sun," while in the language of flowers it signifies "beware of excess."

Crocodiles are supposedly named after the saffron crocus, because the only sincere tears they weep are induced by the beautiful fragrance of this flower.

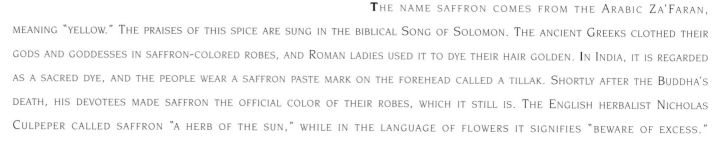

Above *The flower of* Crocus sativus. *The orange stamens can be clearly seen.*

Below *Saffron.*

Origins and Characteristics

Saffron is the world's most expensive spice. It comes from a mauve-colored, autumn-flowering, aromatic crocus from the *iridaceae* family. It is native to Asia, where it is known as *karcom*. It grows about 9 inches high in well-drained, temperate soils. The spice is made from the three orange-colored stigmas that grow in each crocus flower. It is extremely expensive to produce since there is no mechanical means of picking out the fragile stigmas from each individual flower, which must be handpicked. Around 20,000 stigmas are needed to produce a single pound of the spice, so it is just as well that only a small quantity is needed to color food and give flavor. Spanish saffron from La Mancha is now considered to be the best quality.

Flavor and Storage

Saffron has a distinctively pungent, honey-like flavor and aroma, and is available as whole threads or powdered. The threads are the purest saffron, and should be crushed between your fingers when needed, and infused in hot liquid before using. When ground they form a russet powder.

This spice is very sensitive to light, and should be stored in an airtight container out of direct sunlight.

In Asia, turmeric is often mistakenly called saffron, so beware. Because it is so expensive, the powdered form is sometimes adulterated; make sure your supply is pure.

PROPERTIES

Culinary Saffron is used extensively to color rice dishes, sauces, and soups. It is an important ingredient in Spanish *paella* and Indian *pilaus* and *biryani* dishes. A pinch can be added to cream cheese, fish sauces, scrambled eggs, and risotto, or mixed with mayonnaise to add fragrance. It is also good in sweet rice puddings, bread, and cakes. Yeasty saffron buns called saffron cakes are traditionally made once a year in Cornwall in the southwest of England.

Medicinal Saffron is reputedly beneficial for fevers, cramps, and enlarged livers, and may be applied externally for bruises, neuralgia, and rheumatism. It is also considered to be an aphrodisiac, and is slightly narcotic.

Swordfish with Saffron

Any firm white fish is good cooked in this way.

Serves 4

Preparation time 15 minutes, plus marinating.

Cooking time about 15–20 minutes.

Ingredients

1½ lb swordfish steak, cut in chunks

4 tbsp sunflower oil plus extra for cooking

2 tbsp lemon juice

1 cup dry white wine

1 bay leaf

1 thyme sprig

salt and freshly ground black pepper

1 tsp saffron strands

4 tbsp all-purpose flour

2 leeks, thinly sliced

2 carrots, cut into julienne strips

2 celery stalks thinly sliced

1 cup light cream

Preparation

Place fish in a dish. In a jar, combine half the oil, lemon juice, wine, bay leaf, thyme, and seasoning. Shake, then pour it over the fish. Cover and leave to marinate.

Pound the saffron strands to a powder, then stir in 2 tbsp boiling water. Stir until the saffron has dissolved.

Drain the fish, reserving the marinade. Toss fish in the flour, adding a little seasoning. Heat the remaining oil and stir fry the fish until golden brown. Transfer fish to a serving dish and keep hot. Add a little extra oil and stir fry the leeks, carrots, and celery over high heat for 2–3 minutes.

Arrange vegetables with the fish, then pour marinade into pan and boil hard until reduced by half, then reduce the heat and stir in the cream. Add the saffron liquid and heat gently. Do not boil. Spoon the sauce over or around the fish.

CUMIN
Cuminum cyminum

THIS SPICE WAS POPULAR WITH THE ANCIENTS. CUMIN SEEDS HAVE BEEN FOUND IN THE TOMBS OF EGYPTIAN PHARAOHS; IT IS MENTIONED BY THE ROMAN POET HORACE, WHO CALLED IT "EXSANGUE CUMINUM" MEANING "BLOODLESS CUMIN" BECAUSE IT WAS APPLIED TO THE FACE BY WOMEN TO LIGHTEN THEIR COMPLEXION TO MAKE THEM PALE AND INTERESTING; THE GREEKS ASSOCIATED CUMIN WITH MEANNESS; AND MARCUS AURELIUS, WHO WAS ACTUALLY A REMARKABLY ENLIGHTENED ROMAN EMPEROR, WAS NICKNAMED "CUMIN" BY HIS CRITICS, WHO ACCUSED HIM OF AVARICE. THE GERMANS USED TO BAKE BREAD WITH CUMIN SEEDS IN THE BELIEF THAT THIS SPICE WOULD PREVENT IT BEING STOLEN BY WOOD DEMONS. GIRLS HOPED TO KEEP THEIR LOVERS FAITHFUL BY BAKING THEM CUMIN BREAD.

ORIGINS AND CHARACTERISTICS

The cumin plant is a member of the *umbelliferae* family. It is an annual, with divided, threadlike, fragrant leaves, umbels of small pink-white flowers, and aromatic seeds with tiny bristles. It gets its name from the Sanskrit *kamani*, which means "mouse plant." It is indigenous to Egypt, but from very early times cumin has also been cultivated in Arabia and India, where it is called *jerra*. It grows now all over the world, especially in warm climates, but it can also be successfully cultivated in colder environments like Norway.

Often used in veterinary preparations, cumin mixed into flour and water is a good mix for poultry food, and if carrier pigeons eat this spice, they are less likely to stray.

FLAVOR AND STORAGE

The Vietnamese cook with the cumin stems, but it is the seeds that are generally used. They are oval with ridges, and have a nutty aroma and a taste that is bitter, but not hot. When ground, they create a reddish-brown powder. Both seeds and powder need to be stored in airtight containers to keep their flavor. Greater flavor is achieved by making your own powder from roasted whole cumin seeds. To do this, put them into a small cast-iron pan over medium to high heat, and stir until they become darker; they can then be ground to a powder.

Black cumin seeds (*cuminum nigrum*), which are sometimes called "Kashmiri cumin," taste slightly of caraway. This spice, used by the Moguls, grows in Kashmir and Iran. It is very rare, and more expensive than ordinary cumin.

Cumin seed

PROPERTIES

Culinary The Romans used cumin in place of pepper. Popular in Arabic, Indian, Thai, and Cajun cooking, in Europe, it is used to flavor rice, stuffed vegetables, relishes, cordials, and liqueurs such as kümmel. Dutch and Swiss cheeses often have cumin seeds in them. Roasted seeds complement cool yogurts.

Medicinal and cosmetic The essential oil can be added to massage oil to help cellulite problems. An old remedy relates that cumin relieves the stitch if mixed with fine vinegar and applied very hot to the side of the body. In olden times, the powdered seed was applied to the face to give a fashionably pale look. When taken internally, it was believed to be an erotic stimulant. Today, cumin is used in perfumery to enhance other perfumes.

Ground cumin

Lamb and Salt Beef Stew

An unusual one-pot stew using two kinds of meat.

Serves 6

Preparation time 10–15 minutes. Cooking time about 2¼ hours.

Ingredients

½ lb lean salt beef

¼ cup butter or margarine

1 tbsp vegetable oil

2 lb boned lamb or goat, cut into 1-inch pieces

2 cups finely chopped onions

1 large tomato, skinned and chopped

2 tsp peeled and chopped fresh gingerroot

¼ cup chopped green pepper

1 fat garlic clove, chopped

½ fresh chili, chopped

1 tsp salt

2 tsp ground cumin

2 tbsp lime or lemon juice

2½ cups water

3 potatoes, peeled and diced

2 cucumbers, peeled and diced

Preparation

Put salt beef in a saucepan, cover with water, and boil for 30 minutes. Drain and cut into cubes.

Heat the butter or margarine and oil in a large saucepan, then add the lamb or goat and brown it all over. Remove and set to one side. Add onions to the saucepan and cook for 5 minutes. Then add tomato, ginger, green pepper, garlic, chili, salt, and cumin. Cook for 10 minutes, stirring all the time.

Stir in the prepared salt beef, lamb, lime or lemon juice, and the 2½ cups water. Cook for 1 hour over low heat. Add the potatoes and cucumber, and simmer for 20 more minutes.

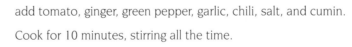

TURMERIC
Curcuma longa

IN THE EAST, TURMERIC IS OFTEN USED AS A DYE, GIVING THE CHARACTERISTIC ORANGE COLOR TO BUDDHIST ROBES. IT WAS ALSO USED AS A BODY PAINT; CHILDREN IN JAVA GOING TO A CIRCUMCISION CEREMONY WERE OFTEN COMPLETELY COVERED WITH THIS SPICE. IN INDONESIA, RICE DYED WITH TURMERIC IS TRADITIONALLY EATEN AT WEDDING FEASTS, AS WELL AS BEING USED TO DYE THE ARMS OF THE BRIDE AND GROOM, WHILE IN INDIA IT IS USED IN RELIGIOUS CEREMONIES. PAPER TINGED WITH TINCTURE OF TURMERIC PROVIDES AN ALKALINITY TEST.

ORIGINS AND CHARACTERISTICS

Turmeric is known as "Salt of the Orient," and has been used since ancient times throughout India and Southeast Asia, where it is known as *yu-chin* or *haldi*. It comes from a perennial plant of the *zingiberaceae* family, and is a relative of ginger. The spice is native to parts of Asia and is cultivated in India, Java, Peru, Sri Lanka, tropical Africa, and the West Indies. It grows to about 3½ feet in height, with large leaves and a cluster of yellow flowers with pink bracts. Its brilliant yellow, cylindrical root is harvested ten months after planting, and is then boiled and dried in ten days to produce the spice. This is polished, either by hand or in a rotating drum, then graded and ground.

Zedoary (*Curcuma zedoaria*), also known as besar, is another member of the *zingiberaceae* family and a type of turmeric. It grows in monsoon areas of the tropics. Its leaves are large, long, and pointed, and grow up sheathed from the base with maroon bands on either side of the midrib. The flowers are pink and yellow, with green and red bracts. The pale yellow rhizome yields a very important essential oil.

FLAVOR AND STORAGE

The dried, aromatic, bright orange root is ground to a brilliant yellow powder, which is not only wonderfully colorful, but also has a pungent, warm, earthy aroma and taste, reminiscent of an Indian bazaar. It is rarely available fresh, but may be bought dried or ground. It should be stored in an airtight container away from the light since, although it will not lose its color, it will lose its flavor.

Turmeric should be handled carefully at all times as it will stain clothes and fingers. It is possible to plant the rhizome in a pot to let it grow so that the leaves can be used, but it is the rhizome that is used as a spice.

Above *Turmeric.*

Left *Turmeric comes from a perennial plant of the* zingiberaceae *family,* Curcuma longa.

PROPERTIES

Culinary Turmeric is an essential spice in much Indian food, transforming drab brown curries and relishes by giving them a rich, appetizing color. It can be used successfully for fish dishes, kedgeree, and deviled eggs. A pinch stirred into a white sauce lends a delicate color and slightly peppery taste, while rice itself takes on a more interesting flavor if boiled in water to which just a tiny amount of turmeric has been added. The spice is widely used in Moroccan cooking, particularly rice dishes, and the British use it in piccalilli and chutneys. However, beware – it should not be used in place of saffron since it has a different taste.

Because turmeric has a strong flavor it should always be used in moderation. The leaves are highly aromatic and are good thrown into soups, but should be removed before serving, in the same way as bay leaves. In Thailand, the young shoots are used as a vegetable. In Indonesia, the leaves of the zedoary variety are used to flavor fish dishes.

Medicinal and cosmetic Research shows turmeric strengthens the gallbladder, inhibits dangerous blood clotting, reduces liver toxins, and helps the liver metabolize fats and so aids weight loss. The Thais also use it for cobra bites. Indian ladies apply turmeric on unwanted facial hair to frustrate its growth, and it is thought that turmeric water gives a golden glow to the complexion. In Biblical times it was used as a perfume, and today slices of dried root from the Zedoary variety are used in perfumery, especially the Indian talc called *abir*.

Rice with Spinach

For this dish, the rice should be freshly cooked.

Serves 4

Preparation time 10 minutes.

Cooking time about 12 minutes, plus cooking rice.

Ingredients

scant 1 cup long-grain rice, cooked

3 tbsp oil

½ small onion, chopped

2 tbsp cumin seeds

1 tsp turmeric

knob of butter (optional)

Preparation

Drain the rice, if necessary. If cooked by the absorption method, do not fork up the grains but leave the pan covered off the heat when the rice is cooked.

Heat the oil and stir fry the onion with the cumin seeds for 5 minutes. Stir in the turmeric and continue to cook for 2 minutes before adding the butter, if used. Let the butter melt, then add the rice and stir fry for 2 minutes until it has become well coated in the flavoring ingredients.

Make a well in the rice or push it to one side of the pan and add the spinach. Stir fry the spinach briefly to heat it through. Then fork the spinach into the rice and serve at once.

LEMON GRASS
Cymbopogon citratus

Oᴵᴸ ᴏꜰ ʟᴇᴍᴏɴ ɢʀᴀss, ᴇxᴛʀᴀᴄᴛᴇᴅ ʙʏ sᴛᴇᴀᴍɪɴɢ, ᴡᴀs ᴜsᴇᴅ ᴛᴏ ᴛʀᴇᴀᴛ ᴄʜᴏʟᴇʀᴀ. Aʟᴛʜᴏᴜɢʜ ɪᴛ ɪs sᴛɪʟʟ ɪᴍᴘᴏʀᴛᴀɴᴛ ɪɴ Iɴᴅɪᴀɴ ᴀʏᴜʀᴠᴇᴅɪᴄ ᴍᴇᴅɪᴄɪɴᴇ, ɪᴛ ɪs ʜᴀʀᴅʟʏ ᴜsᴇᴅ ɪɴ Wᴇsᴛᴇʀɴ ʜᴇʀʙᴀʟɪsᴍ.

ORIGINS AND CHARACTERISTICS

Lemon grass is a species of citronella. This grass has bulbous stems, which become leaf blades, then a branched panicle of flowers. It thrives on sandy soil in hot climates with plenty of rain, reaching about 5 feet in height. The long grass blades are blue-green and smell strongly of lemon. The 4–6 inches of leek-like stalks have a very succulent flavor. If you slice a fresh stalk, you can see concentric sheathed leaves inside. The highest-quality lemon grass is still found in its indigenous home on the Malabar coast near the ancient Indian spice port of Cochin, although it is now cultivated in Southeast Asia and South America. Its colloquial name is Indian Verbena.

FLAVOR AND STORAGE

The slender shoots of lemon grass smell and taste of lemon due to the presence of citric oils. This spice is available dried or in a powdered form called "sereh powder." Ground lemon grass does not have the fibrous quality of fresh lemon grass, which is difficult to chew. They are both best kept in airtight glass jars.

PROPERTIES

Culinary Lemon grass provides one of the characteristic flavors in Thai, Indonesian, Vietnamese, and Malaysian cooking. The chopped stalks combine particularly well with fish dishes, stir fries, and curries, but as they remain very tough even after cooking, they need to be well pounded first if they are going to be eaten. They can also be chopped into salads, and can be added to syrup for fruit or sorbet.

Medicinal and cosmetic Lemon grass is traditionally taken as a tea to relieve flatulence, the symptoms of colds and flu, and as an antiseptic. The essential oil is used in cosmetics and in aromatherapy to improve circulation and ease muscle pain. It will also treat athlete's foot and acne, and, sprayed into the air, it reduces airborne infections.

Above *Lemon grass*, Cymbopogon citratus.

Beef Crystal Spring Rolls

If lemon grass is unavailable, use the juice of a lemon and its grated rind.

Serves 4

Preparation time 25 minutes, plus marinating.

Cooking time 2–3 minutes per batch of meat.

Ingredients

Marinade

1 tsp lemon grass, finely minced

1 tsp garlic, finely minced

1 tbsp ginger wine

½ lb steak, cut against the grain into piece ⅛ inch thick and 2 inches long

6 oz rice vermicelli

2 pickled onions, finely chopped

2 dill pickles, finely chopped

1 carrot, grated

1 packet round Banh Trang rice paper

Dipping Sauce

4 tbsp Nuoc Mam sauce or Maggi liquid seasoning

1 red chili pepper, finely chopped

1 garlic clove, finely chopped

1 tbsp lime or lemon juice

1 tsp wine vinegar

1 tsp sugar

2 tsp dry sherry

To Serve

1 Boston lettuce

coriander and mint sprigs

Preparation

Combine the marinade ingredients together and marinate the steak slices for 2–3 hours.

Soak the rice vermicelli. When soft, drain thoroughly. Toss the cold rice vermicelli, pickled onion, pickles, and carrot together and place on the table in a dish.

Prepare the dipping sauce by mixing all dipping ingredients together and stir well. Put the lettuce leaves in a dish, the coriander, and mint on a flat plate, and place on the table. Put the rice paper on a plate and place on the table.

Put warm water in a bowl that is large enough for the rice paper to be dipped in on the table. Put either a table-top barbecue or a fondue on the table and bring the marinated meat to the table for the guests to cook. If neither is available, broil the meat very quickly, or fry in a pan with a little vegetable oil. Either way the cooking time is minimal, as thinly cut meat cooks extremely quickly. Excessive cooking toughens the meat.

Guests should help themselves by dipping a rice paper into the warm water until it becomes soft and pliable. They then place some of the vermicelli and pickle, mint, and coriander and the cooked pieces of beef on the rice paper. The mixture is then rolled up and placed on a fresh piece of lettuce. The lettuce leaf is rolled around it and then dipped in the sauce.

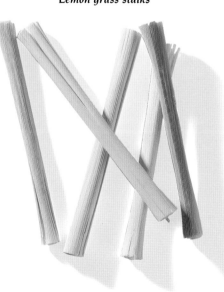

Lemon grass stalks

Ground lemon grass

CARDAMOM
Elettaria cardamomum

IN SAUDI ARABIA THEY DRINK A CARDAMOM COFFEE, SOMETIMES FLAVORED WITH CLOVES, CALLED GAHIRA. IT IS IMPORTANT IN CEREMONIAL HOSPITALITY, AND IS USED TO PROMOTE TRANQUILITY BEFORE ANY BUSINESS IS DISCUSSED. THE HOST MUST POUR THE COFFEE HIMSELF AND THE GUEST IS EXPECTED TO DRINK SEVERAL CUPS.

ORIGINS AND CHARACTERISTICS

Cardamom is from the *zingiberaceae* family and is a relative of ginger. It is the dried, unripened fruit of a perennial plant that grows about 10 feet high in India's tropical forests. Its local name is *elaychi*, and Indians honor it as the "Queen of Spices," pepper being "king." The plant has white flowers with violet stripes, and at intervals during the summer it produces green pods containing dark reddish-brown seeds. These must be harvested before they split open and are then laid out to be dried in the sun. Cardamom is now grown in several places worldwide, including Sri Lanka, Central America, and Thailand. It is difficult to cultivate, however, so inferior varieties of cardamom pods are often sold.

Above Dried cardamom pods.
Below The flowers of Elettaria cardamomum are white with violet stripes.

FLAVOR AND STORAGE

Cardamom has a sweet, lemony, eucalyptus flavor. It is available as a powder, dried pods, or loose seeds. It is best to buy the whole pod, and then extract and crush the seeds before use. The seeds are very hard and need to be cracked by pressure with a rolling pin. Cardamom should be always stored in an airtight container. Inferior cardamom has a stronger taste.

PROPERTIES.

Culinary Cardamom is most popular in Indian curries, but is also used in Scandinavian dishes. A teaspoon of crushed seeds put into the dry pastry mix before adding the liquid gives a superb flavor. The whole cardamom pod is delightful in fruity sweet dishes, ice cream, and custards, but should be removed before serving. It is often combined with almonds and saffron. This spice can be used to flavor tea, and some ground seed mixed with sugar is great with black coffee; it is also used in mulled wine.

Ground cardamom

Medicinal and cosmetic Cardamom is said to have a cooling effect on the body. It is good for skin disorders, coughing, piles, jaundice, headaches, fever, all digestive disorders, and is used as a slimming aid. If chewed after meals, cardamom seeds will sweeten the breath.

The ancient Egyptians used this spice as a tooth whitener and breath freshener. Cardamom and sesame were dedicated by the ancients to the deities Circe, Medea, and Hecate. Hecate became the goddess of witches, and so cardamom developed an ill-deserved association with evil in the popular imagination. It is renowned as a powerful aphrodisiac. In France, cardamom oil is used in perfumery and some scented domestic articles.

Rich Cardamom Cookies

These rich butter cookies are flavored with cardamom, a favorite Scandinavian spice.

Makes about 24

Preparation time 20 minutes.

Cooking time 12–14 minutes.

Ingredients

2 cups cake flour

4 tsp ground cardamom

¼ tsp salt

¾ cup (1½ sticks) unsalted butter, softened

½ cup superfine sugar

½ cup sliced or flaked almonds

To Decorate

⅓ cup confectioners' sugar

1½ tsp cardamom

sliced or flaked almonds

Preparation

Grease 2 large baking sheets. Into a medium bowl, sift together the flour, cardamom, and salt.

In a large bowl with an electric mixer, beat the butter until creamy, 30 seconds. Gradually add the sugar and continue beating until light and fluffy, 1–2 minutes. On low speed, gradually beat in the flour mixture until well blended; then stir in the sliced or flaked almonds.

Into a small bowl, sift together confectioners' sugar and cardamom. Using a tablespoon, scoop out the dough and roll into roughly 1½-inch balls. Then drop these balls one at a time into the sugar-spice mixture, rolling to coat them well. Then place them 1½ inches apart on the baking sheets. Dip the bottom of a glass into the sugar mixture, and flatten the cookies to ½-inch thick rounds. Press 2 or 3 sliced or flaked almonds onto the tops of the cookies for decoration.

Bake the cookies at 375°F until golden brown. This should take 12–14 minutes. Make sure you rotate the baking sheets from top to bottom shelf and from front to back halfway through cooking time. Remove the baking sheets to wire racks to cool for 2–3 minutes. Then, using a thin metal palette knife, carefully remove the cookies to wire racks to cool completely. Store in airtight containers.

CLOVES
Eugenia caryophyllus

Cloves have an attractive aroma, and used to be burned in wealthy households to sweeten the air. Cloves have always been expensive, and remain so today. In 1265, Eleanor Countess of Leicester, wife of the English soldier and statesman Simon De Montfort recorded spending 12 shillings for a pound of cloves, a small fortune in today's money.

ORIGINS AND CHARACTERISTICS

Whole cloves are the dried, unopened buds of a tropical evergreen tree from the myrtle family, which grows about 30 feet high and produces aromatic pink flowers twice a year. Before they open, they are harvested by beating the branches, then dried in the sun, where they turn a dark reddish brown. Clove trees can go on bearing for 100 years. They are native to the Moluccas, which is now part of Indonesia, and the importance of cloves helped earn these isles the nickname of "The Spice Islands." They were introduced from there to Penang, Amboyna, and Madagascar. Zanzibar is the major source of cloves today. The name of this spice is derived from the Latin *clavus* meaning "nail," which the clove resembles.

FLAVOR AND STORAGE

Cloves have a distinctive spicy aroma and taste. When eaten, it is as if their bouquet of pungent sweetness was being absorbed through the roof of the mouth. All cloves do not retain their flavor long and should be kept in an airtight jar in a dry, dark environment.

Above *Cloves are the dried, unopened buds of the tropical evergreen tree* Eugenia caryophyllus.
Below *Ground cloves.*

PROPERTIES

Culinary Traditionally, cloves are used to flavor apple pies, mincemeat, hot cross buns, mulled wines, stewed fruit, meat dishes, curries, and soups. For soups, a whole onion can be studded with cloves, simmered along with the other ingredients, then removed before serving.

In Italy, cloves are used in candied walnuts, and in India they form an important ingredient of *garam masala* curry powder. The Germans make a spice bread with clove. Over half of the world's clove production, however, goes to Indonesia to produce clove cigarettes.

Medicinal Oil of cloves is a powerful antiseptic, found in toothpastes and mouthwash. During the Han Dynasty in China, subjects were expected to approach their emperor with cloves in their mouth, to sweeten their breath. The Chinese still use cloves as a mild anaesthetic for toothache. Some people, however, find that eating cloves can inflame the intestinal lining, which is particularly bad for anyone with an ulcer.

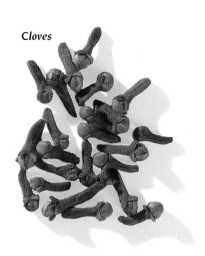

Cloves

Roast Pork Calypso

Flavored with onion, the pork is marinated for tender results.

Serves 6

Ingredients

4 lb piece of pork

2 cups cold water

1 tbsp vinegar

1 tbsp salt

3 garlic cloves, crushed

1 tsp thyme

1 onion, grated

1 tsp ground cloves

1 tbsp chopped fresh parsley

Preparation

Place pork in a saucepan, cover with water and add vinegar, salt, garlic, and thyme. Marinate for several hours.

Meanwhile, mix the onion, cloves, and parsley in a bowl. When the pork is ready, remove it from the saucepan and make 2-inch long gashes all over. Fill the holes with the onion mixture. Pour the marinade into a baking dish.

Lay the pork in the dish and roast at 160°F for about 2½ hours until cooked.

Preparation time 15 minutes, plus marinating. Cooking time about 30 minutes.

ASAFETIDA
Ferula assa-foetida, F. *narthex*

Below *Asafetida*, Ferula assa-foetida, *in flower.*

ASAFETIDA IS A SPICE WITH A PUNGENT SMELL OF ROTTEN EGGS, WHICH EXPLAINS ITS COMMON NAMES OF DEVIL'S DUNG AND STINKING GUM. DESPITE THIS, THE MILKY SAP OF THE PLANT FROM WHICH IT IS TAKEN IS USED IN THE MANUFACTURE OF INCENSE.

ORIGINS AND CHARACTERISTICS

Asafetida is a resin taken from a handsome plant with a thick rootstock, feather foliage, and small flowers ranging from light yellow to dark brown. The sap is collected by cutting the stalk off at the root. The sap then solidifies, and can be ground into a powder. Asafetida is found in Afghanistan, China, and Russia.

FLAVOR AND STORAGE

Asafetida has a very strong smell of rotten eggs, but this turns to an oniony smell when the spice is heated. It comes as a blackish lump sold in pieces, or as a grainy powder. The lump is regarded as purer, but it may be easier to buy ground. To crush your own powder, chip small amounts from the lump with a hammer, and crush them between pieces of paper. Store in an airtight container in a cool, dry environment.

PROPERTIES

Culinary Asafetida is used almost exclusively in Iranian and Indian cooking, especially vegetarian dishes; it is included as much for its digestive qualities as for its taste. It is a strong spice that should be used sparingly. Asafetida is a popular replacement for onions among certain Hindu Brahmins and Jains, who are not only strict vegetarians, but also refrain from eating onions and garlic. It is an important ingredient of an Indian snack called *cheewra*—a mixture of grains, dried fruits, and spices. This spice is also found in Indian relishes such as *maulka pori*, and is an ingredient of Worcestershire sauce, and a little can be added to flavor fish and vegetable dishes.

Medicinal Asafetida can be taken in the form of a gum and is said to aid digestion, nervous disorders, bronchitis, and asthma. Some believe it is an anticoagulant, which may lower blood pressure. This spice also finds a role in some forms of veterinary medicine.

Asafetida

FENNEL
Foeniculum vulgare

FENNEL IS CONSIDERED A VERY MAGICAL PLANT IN MYTHS AND LEGENDS OF THE MEDITERRANEAN, WHERE IT ORIGINATED, AND IN MANY OTHER COUNTRIES. THE ANGLO-SAXONS REGARDED IT AS ONE OF THE NINE SACRED HERBS. IN FOLKLORE, IT IS SAID TO KEEP THE EVIL EYE AT BAY. FENNEL FORMS PART OF AN INDIAN LOVE POTION DESCRIBED AS "HOLY AND PARTAKING OF THE ESSENCE OF NECTAR."

Above *Fennel*, Foeniculum vulgare, *grows as high as 6½ feet tall.*

ORIGINS AND CHARACTERISTICS

Fennel, sometimes known as "finocchio," originates in the Mediterranean, but is now grown worldwide, especially in Egypt, India, and the Far East. It is also cultivated for export in Germany, Italy, and France. The variety used as a spice is not the wild type. The plant grows in most conditions, but prefers a sunny, sheltered spot. It grows as high as 6½ feet, and has a thick root, feathery leaves, umbels of yellow flowers, and curved, ribbed seeds, which are harvested just before they ripen. When dried, the pale green seeds turn a light beige color.

FLAVOR AND STORAGE

Fennel seeds taste like celery with a slight aniseed flavor. They can be bought whole or powdered; the whole seeds can be roasted to increase their flavor. The foliage is not recommended for drying, but can be used fresh. Fennel is used as a substitute for dill. It soon loses its flavor, however, and should not be kept too long. Store it in an airtight container, in a cool, dry place away from the light.

PROPERTIES

Culinary The dried seed powder is excellent on poached eggs and in all sauces. It can also add taste to apple pies, custards, and other desserts, as well as piquant dishes such as curries, soups, and certain breads. Branches of leaves are traditionally used to cover fish when baking, while red mullet barbecued on a bed of fennel is a French specialty. The fat bulb root has a superb flavor, and makes a delicious addition to a salad when finely chopped. It can be cooked as a vegetable and served with butter or cheese—a favorite Italian dish (see opposite). Italians also like fennel with roast pork and add it to *finocchiona*, a salami from Florence. Fennel oil is used in pickles and condiments.

Medicinal Fennel was considered to be a very important medicine in the past. It was noted by the herbalist, Culpeper, that fennel seeds were used in medicines for wheezing and shortness of breath. Whole fennel seeds are chewed to freshen the breath. Reputed to eliminate poisons and reduce gas, they are excellent for stomach upsets. For this reason they are often added to the cooking water of greens such as brussel sprouts. They are an ingredient of *pa'an*, an Indian digestive. In ancient China and India, fennel was used as a remedy for snakebites and scorpion stings. The feathery foliage is used as a garnish on food, and is beneficial to the brain and memory. Fennel is also said to help eyesight, and in folklore to increase "second-sight." Fennel seed teas are often recommended in weight-loss programs. The athletes of ancient Greece ate fennel to keep down their weight and boost their strength.

Fennel seed

Baked Fennel

Florence fennel, or finocchio, is a root vegetable with a pleasant anise flavor. Here it is boiled first in chicken stock, then baked with Parmesan cheese.

Serves 4

Preparation time 10 minutes. Cooking time 22–25 minutes.

Ingredients

1 large or 2 small fennel bulbs (about 1½ lb)

3 cups chicken stock

salt and pepper

2 tbsp butter

¼ cup freshly grated Parmesan cheese

The fat bulb root

Preparation

Trim off the fennel stems and discard. Cut the bulb into wedges. Bring the chicken stock to a boil in a medium saucepan. Add the fennel and boil until the fennel is barely tender, about 12 minutes. Drain the fennel.

Arrange the fennel in a buttered casserole. Season with salt and pepper. Dot with butter and sprinkle with Parmesan cheese. Bake at 350°F for about 10 minutes until the cheese is melted.

Star anise seed

Above Illicium verum *has shiny leaves and white flowers.*

Star anise, broken pieces

STAR ANISE
Illicium verum

STAR ANISE IS REDDISH BROWN IN COLOR AND SHAPED LIKE AN IRREGULAR, EIGHT-POINTED STAR. IN FACT, ITS CHINESE NAME MEANS EIGHT POINTS. IT IS A PRETTY SPICE THAT CAN BE USED CREATIVELY TO MAKE ATTRACTIVE DECORATIONS.

ORIGINS AND CHARACTERISTICS

Star Anise is the fruit of a small Chinese tree now grown throughout Southeast Asia, with yellow flowers and shiny green leaves. Not surprisingly, because of their attractive appearance, the leaves are used in potpourri, as are the scented leaves of anise hyssop, a North American relative of the aniseed family. The oil of Japanese star anise is used in soaps and hair oils.

FLAVOR AND STORAGE

Star anise smells strongly of aniseed, although it is not related. It has a more liquorice-like aroma than aniseed. However, it is rich in anethole, an essential oil also found in aniseed, so it is often used as a substitute for this more familiar spice. It is available whole or ground, and should be stored in an airtight container away from sunlight.

PROPERTIES

Culinary Star anise has many culinary uses, especially in Chinese cooking. It is good in fish stews, excellent with cabbage, and can also be used in candies, cakes, and desserts such as rice pudding. It is excellent with spicy fruit desserts, combining particularly well with peaches, plums, nectarines, and cherries. It is one of the spices used to create Chinese five-spice powder. The flower of star anise is used to flavor vermouth and liqueurs.

Ground star anise

Star anise, whole

Spicy Beef Stew

A tender beef dish with an Oriental flavor.

Serves 4

Preparation time 15 minutes. Cooking time about 2 hours.

Ingredients

3 tbsp vegetable oil

2 medium onions, finely chopped

5 garlic cloves, finely chopped

10 scallions, trimmed

1 stalk lemon grass, cut into 2-inch sections and crushed

2 lb stewing beef, cut into 1-inch cubes

5 cups water

½ cup yellow bean sauce, chopped and crushed

1 tsp chili powder

4 star anise

1-inch cinnamon stick

½ tsp whole peppercorns

sugar

Preparation

Heat 1 tbsp of the oil in a wok over a medium high heat. Put in the onions, garlic, and whole scallions and stir fry for 2 minutes. Then add the lemon grass and continue to stir until the onions become lightly brown. When this is done, remove the scallions and set aside.

Heat the remaining oil over a high heat. Stir fry as many pieces of beef as possible until they are brown, turning them over from time to time. Continue until all the beef has been cooked.

Add the water. Add the lemon grass mixture, yellow bean sauce, chili powder, star anise, cinnamon, peppercorns, and sugar, and bring to a boil. Cover and lower the heat to simmer gently for 1½ hours.

Add the reserved scallions, cover again and let simmer for a further 15 minutes or until the sauce has thickened a little and the meat is tender.

Juniper berries

JUNIPER
Juniperus communis

IN THE OLD TESTAMENT WE ARE TOLD THAT IT WAS A JUNIPER TREE THAT SHELTERED THE PROPHET ELIJAH FROM THE WRATH OF KING AHAB. SIMILARLY, A CHRISTIAN LEGEND RELATES THAT DURING THE FLIGHT INTO EGYPT, HEROD'S MEN CAME VERY CLOSE TO CAPTURING THE HOLY FAMILY AND IN DESPERATION MARY TRIED TO HIDE THE BABY JESUS AMONG SOME TREES. IMMEDIATELY A JUNIPER MAGICALLY OPENED ITS BRANCHES AND CONCEALED THE BABY. FOR THIS REASON, THE JUNIPER TREE IS DEDICATED TO THE VIRGIN MARY, AND AT CHRISTMAS IN ITALY IT IS HUNG UP AS A DECORATION IN THE SAME WAY THAT OTHER COUNTRIES USE HOLLY.

ORIGINS AND CHARACTERISTICS

Below *The berries of* Juniperus communis *take two to three years to ripen.*

Juniper is an evergreen tree of the *cupressaceae* family that flourishes in the northern hemisphere. There are many varieties, but the type yielding the best spice is native to the Mediterranean, arctic Norway, and Russia. These trees grow about 33 feet tall, but the North American *Juniperus virginiana* can grow as high as 100 feet.

Juniper trees have needle-like leaves that grow in threes. Male and female flowers are borne on separate plants; these are yellowish green in color and appear in late spring or summer. The small, fleshy, three-sided berries take two or three years to ripen to a black-purplish blue. While the berries are ripening, new small cones are growing on the tree at the same time.

FLAVOR AND STORAGE

Juniper berries have a spicy smell and bittersweet flavor with a peppery aftertaste. They are available fresh or dry, and should be stored in a sealed container, where they will last for about six months before the flavor fades. Generally six to nine berries are required for cooking. They should be crushed first with the back of a spoon.

PROPERTIES

Culinary Juniper is used with rich meats, and is almost essential with game dishes. It is excellent with domestic poultry, and can be put into stuffing. Crushed or whole dried berries are traditionally used in pickling meats, marinades, pâtés, sauces, and conserves. The Germans love them in coleslaw and sauerkraut. Juniper berries are also used as a spice to flavor bitters and liqueurs, especially gin, which takes its name from juniper: "ginepro," "geniever," or "genever." It is used commercially to flavor cola and chewing gum.

Medicinal and cosmetic Juniper oil is said to be good for cystitis, kidney complaints, acne, eczema, rheumatism, cellulite, and is used as a diuretic. Fresh juniper leaves treat blisters. In the past, its chief use was in cases of dropsy occurring from heart, liver, or kidney diseases. Juniper should not be taken during pregnancy, however, as it could cause a miscarriage. In Africa, it was thought to have antivenereal properties. Native Americans burned the needles as incense, and in European folklore juniper berries were burned at funerals to banish evil spirits, and by housewives in the home to rid the house of demons. Today, juniper is used as a fragrance in perfumes, soaps, and detergents.

Garlic Roasted Duck

The duck portions are first marinated, then roasted.

Serves 4

Preparation time 10–15 minutes, plus marinating.

Cooking time 1 hour.

Ingredients

1 tbsp Nuoc Mam sauce or light soy sauce

⅔ cup red wine vinegar

1 onion, chopped

12 juniper berries, crushed

2 tsp fennel seeds

1 garlic clove, crushed

4 duck breast and wing portions

½ cup yogurt

salt and freshly ground black pepper

watercress, to garnish

Preparation

Mix the Nuoc Mam sauce, vinegar, onion, juniper berries, fennel seeds, and garlic in a large bowl and rub well into the duck. Cover the bowl with some plastic wrap and leave in a refrigerator for 8 hours, turning occasionally.

Drain and reserve the marinade. Place the duck portions, skin side down, in an ovenproof dish. Cook at 425°F for 30 minutes, basting at least once. Turn the duck portions over, baste and cook for a further 30 minutes, basting at least once. Switch off the oven but leave the duck in it.

Spoon 1 cup of the marinade into a hot pan, cover and let simmer for at least 5 minutes. Strain, whisk in the yogurt and season with salt and pepper to taste.

Serve the duck on a dish garnished with the watercress. The sauce is served in a bowl. If guests are not proficient with chopsticks, the duck should be chopped into bite-sized pieces.

AMCHOOR
Mangifera indica

MANGO FRUIT IS EATEN RAW, CANDIED, AND PICKLED. THE AMCHOOR SPICE IS OBTAINED BY GRINDING SLICES OF UNRIPE MANGO THAT HAVE BEEN DRIED TO BECOME LIGHT BROWN IN COLOR.

ORIGINS AND CHARACTERISTICS

Amchoor is an Indian spice also known as mango powder. It comes from the mango tree, which grows fast, producing large panicles of fragrant, greenish-white flowers. Each year it yields one or sometimes two crops of large, musk-scented fruit, with a tough yellow, red, or green skin, and pinkish flesh inside. The spice is made by drying and grinding peeled slices of tart, unripe mango into a fine powder.

FLAVOR AND STORAGE

Amchoor has a sour, lemony taste, with a slightly sweet edge. A souring agent, it makes a good substitute for tamarind pulp, lemons, and limes. Amchoor is available in powdered form from ethnic Indian stores. It should be stored in an airtight container away from light.

Above Mangifera indica *produces large panicles of fragrant, greenish-white flowers.*

PROPERTIES

Culinary Amchoor is added to vegetarian curries to add piquancy, as well as to Indian *samosas* (a fried meat-, chicken-, and vegetable-filled type of turnover) and relishes. It is used as a dry seasoning for grilled dishes and sometimes appears in Bombay mix, the Indian version of potato chips or pretzels. It can also be used with chickpeas, potatoes, and eggplant.

Medicinal The bark is used in India for the treatment of internal bleeding and to tone the gums. The ash of burned leaves is applied to burns.

Dry mango slices

Amchoor, mango powder

Curry Leaf
Murraya koenigii

The beautiful white and golden-colored flowers of this Asian plant are a perfect addition to potpourri. The small leaves give off a curry-like odor when bruised, but the leaves when dried have virtually no flavor in comparison with a stalk of fresh leaves.

Origins and Characteristics

Curry leaf comes from a small shrub of the *rutaceae* family. It is a relative of the orange, native to Asia, where it is known as *karapincha*. The plant grows up to 20 feet high, and has large panicles of white or golden-colored flowers. The leaves are shaped like small bay leaves.

Below Murraya koenigii *is a small shrub of the* rutaceae *family.*

Flavor and Storage

These aromatic leaves are named after their curry smell, and are available fresh or dried. Fresh leaves are more aromatic, and can be kept in a plastic bag in the refrigerator for about two weeks; they can also be frozen. Dried leaves quickly lose a lot of their flavor and aroma, but can be used if fresh are unavailable. Store the dried leaves in a screwtop jar in a dark, dry place.

Properties

Culinary Curry leaves are usually used whole in Indian dishes, such as curries, when a milder taste is desired. They are especially popular in southern India and Sri Lanka, but are generally removed before serving since they can cause stomach upsets.

Dried curry leaves

Medicinal The cosmetic bark of orange jasmine (*murraya paniculata*) is a member of this family. It has aromatic, citrus-scented leaves and bark, jasmine-perfumed flowers, and decorative red berries. The leaves are used to help menstrual problems and gonorrhea. The leaves and roots are used as a sedative, and to boost blood circulation.

Whole nutmeg

Below Myristica fragrans *produces* *both nutmeg and mace.*

NUTMEG AND MACE
Myristica fragrans

AT ONE TIME NUTMEGS WERE SO FASHIONABLE PEOPLE WORE THEM AS A NECKLACE AND CARRIED A GRATER. IN AMERICA, A CONMAN ONCE CASHED IN ON THEIR POPULARITY BY PASSING OFF SO MANY FALSE "NUTMEGS" MADE OF WHITTLED WOOD, THAT HE EARNED THE STATE OF CONNECTICUT THE NICKNAME "THE NUTMEG STATE."

ORIGINS AND CHARACTERISTICS

Nutmeg and mace both come from the same 30-foot tropical tree found in Sri Lanka, Malaya, the Molucca Islands, and Sumatra. The outside of the tree's fruit is a shell, and inside is a smooth, hard nut with a crimson lacy covering, called aril. This covering is removed and dried in the sun for a few hours, which turns it pale and brittle. This is mace. Inside the hard, black nut is a kernel that is nutmeg. Nutmegs differ from country to country, so the shape and flavor vary. They get their name from a 14th-century description *nux moschata*, meaning "musk-scented nut." The name "mace" derives from the 14th-century French word maci, meaning "suitable for an ointment."

By the late Middle Ages these spices were very valuable, mace more so than nutmeg. It was said that a pound of mace would purchase three sheep. The Dutch colonists controlled a monopoly of nutmeg and mace production, and tried to prevent anyone else growing or selling the spices; in 1760 they had such large stocks that they burned huge quantities in order to keep prices high. This monopoly lasted until the British occupation of the Moluccas in 1796. It was then grown in Penang and eventually in the New World tropics, where it is now a successful commercial commodity in the world market.

FLAVOR AND STORAGE

Ground nutmeg

Nutmeg has a more robust flavor than mace, but they are otherwise very similar—a warm, rich flavor that does not dominate other flavorings. It is far better to buy whole nutmegs and grate them with a nutmeg grater when needed, rather than buy ground nutmeg, which loses its flavor very quickly. The hard, dried nutmeg is big for a seed, and should be kept in a small, airtight jar.

Mace can be dried into a powder or used whole. Whole mace is known as a "blade" of mace, and is more golden in color than nutmeg. Mace is more refined in taste than nutmeg, and has a stronger flavor, so less is needed in cooking. Both are best added at the end of cooking so as to capture their fragrance.

PROPERTIES

Culinary Grated nutmeg is excellent in custards, cakes, biscuits, pumpkin pie, soups, breads, and practically all milky drinks. The Dutch add a grind of nutmeg to mashed potatoes, cabbage, and rice dishes. Mace is used in sausages, catsup, creamed spinach, sauces for fish, pickle chutney, cheese dishes, carrots, and creamed potatoes. It is also great in avocado soup and kipper pâté, and essential in potted shrimps.

Mace blades

Medicinal The Indians consider nutmeg one of their finest medicines, a cure-all. Ayurvedic medicine uses nutmeg for easing fevers and headaches. In correct doses it helps epileptic convulsions, but an excess of nutmeg can cause myristicin poisoning, which starts off with hallucinations and can be fatal. In the Sixties, "nutmeg parties" were all the rage, and nutmegs were put into drinks as hallucinogens. The effect lasted up to six hours, and took 24 hours to recover from.

In folklore, grated nutmeg mixed with lard is a remedy for piles, and a whole nutmeg carried in the pocket can cure rheumatism and prevent boils. To dream of nutmeg is said to foretell impending changes. In the Orient it was highly prized as an aphrodisiac.

Grenadian ground mace

Rice Pudding

This rich rice pudding has spices and raisins added.

Serves 6

Preparation time 15 minutes. Cooking time 1 hour.

Ingredients

1½ cups milk

2 tbsp butter, melted

4 eggs, lightly beaten

6 tbsp sugar

1 tsp vanilla extract

1 tsp grated lemon rind

½ tsp cinnamon

¼ tsp grated nutmeg

½ cup raisins

1½ cups cooked rice

Preparation

In a large bowl, mix all the ingredients together, except the rice: spices have a tendency to clump, so use a wire whisk. Stir in the rice.

Pour into a buttered casserole dish and bake at 325°F, stirring once after 15 minutes, until the custard sets, about 1 hour. Serve warm.

MYRTLE
Myrtus communis

SWEET MYRTLE IS USED AS PART OF BRIDAL WREATHS AS A SYMBOL OF CHASTITY AND BEAUTY. CONVERSELY, IN THE MIDDLE AGES, HOWEVER, IT WAS TAKEN WITH WHITE WINE AS A "GOOD CORDIAL THAT INCLINES THOSE WHO DRINK IT TO BE VERY AMOROUS."

Below *Both the leaves and berries of* Myrtus communis *are used in cooking.*

ORIGINS AND CHARACTERISTICS

Myrtle is a dense evergreen shrub that grows to about 17 feet. It flourishes in well-drained soil in the sunny Mediterranean and North Africa. The fragrant leaves are dark, shiny green with deeply embedded oil glands. It has creamy white flowers and blue-black berries, which are ground to form a kind of pepper. It is sometimes known as sweet myrtle. Tarentina is a narrow-leaved, compact form of myrtle.

FLAVOR AND STORAGE

Myrtle flower buds and berries give an orange-blossom scent to sweet dishes. The berries should be stored in an airtight container which should then be kept in a cool, dry environment.

PROPERTIES

Culinary Myrtle berries are used in sweet dishes, while the leaves are used in the same way as bay leaves, adding flavor and aroma to roasted meat, as well as stews and ragouts.

Medicinal and cosmetic Myrtle leaves are said to be antiseptic and astringent, and are used in decoction on bruises and hemorrhoids. The leaf essential oil is prescribed for gingivitis. The flowers are made into toilet water called *eau d'ange*. The leaves and flowers together are dried for potpourri, and are also added to blemish ointments.

NIGELLA
Nigella sativa

ALTHOUGH NOT RELATED TO THE ONION FAMILY, THESE SEEDS RESEMBLE ONION SEEDS, HENCE THIS SPICE'S COLLOQUIAL NAME "BLACK ONION SEED."

ORIGINS AND CHARACTERISTICS

Nigella is a small, irregular-shaped black seed of a hardy annual plant that grows wild in India, where it is known as *kalonji*. As well as in India, it is cultivated in Egypt and the Middle East, where it is called *si jah-davels*. A mature plant is about 12 inches high, with feathery foliage, gray-blue flowers, and inflated pods of black seeds. The delicate flowers are surrounded by even more delicate lacy bracts. The fruit is formed of united follicles.

FLAVOR AND STORAGE

Nigella has a strawberry scent and a peppery, nutmeg-like taste. It is available in Indian and Middle Eastern grocery stores in larger city centers, and should be stored in an airtight container.

Above Nigella sativa *grows* 12 *inches high, with abundant flowers and feathery foliage.*

PROPERTIES

Culinary This spice can be used fresh or dry-roasted in curries, and added to vegetables, pulses, relishes, and yogurts. It is excellent spinkled onto Indian, Turkish, and Middle Eastern breads. It is featured in many spice mixtures such as the Bengali five-spice mixture *panchphoron*, which also includes fenugreek, mustard, cumin, and fennel.

Medicinal In India, nigella is used to repel lice from clothes and eaten to treat intestinal worms and nerve problems. It is also said to induce sweating, reduces flatulence, and stimulates milk flow in mothers. The warm ground seed was once thought to restore a lost sense of smell, and was sniffed in a sweet powder form like snuff.

Nigella seed

SCREWPINE
Pandanus odoratissimus

In India, the leaves of the screwpine tree are sacred to the god Shiva. The aromatic leaves are also tossed into wells in order to scent the water.

ORIGINS AND CHARACTERISTICS

Screwpine is part of the *pandanacea* family, and it grows in marshy coastal areas, mainly in Southeast Asia. The tree reaches some 20 feet in height, and, when mature, produces scented white bracts around the male flower and pineapple-like fruit.

Pandanus latifolius, known as *rampe*, is a variety of screwpine grown in Sri Lanka. It is a shrub-like tree cultivated for its aromatic young leaves, which are a very bright green. *Pandanus veitchii*, another variety, is a variegated shrub with long, pointed leaves.

FLAVOR AND STORAGE

The long, flat leaves are either boiled or crushed to yield a distinctive flavor, somewhat like strong almond. They can be bought dried, and should be kept in a dry, airtight jar.

PROPERTIES

Culinary Screwpine is as popular in the East as vanilla is in the West, and is used in the same way to flavor candies and desserts. It is used in Thai, Malaysian, and Indonesian cooking, particularly in rice dishes. The leaves have the decorative effect of coloring food green. They are sometimes cooked in a syrup, which is then strained and added to a dish. The floral essence, reminiscent of rose, is added to both sweet and spicy dishes. The fragrant, savory, evergreen leaves of *pandanus latifolius* are added fresh or dried to Asian recipes. The bracts around the male flower contain a strong, rose-scented essential oil, used in Indian dishes and fragrant waters.

Medicinal and cosmetic Screwpine leaves are used in Asian medicine as a cure for leprosy, syphilis, and scabies. The essential oil is antiseptic and stimulating, often being prescribed in Nepal for headaches and rheumatism. It is also a popular ingredient in Indian perfumes.

Above *Part of the* pandanacea *family, the name of screwpine,* Pandanus odoratissimus, *reflects the spiral arrangement of the leaves.*

POPPY

Papaver somniferum

The ancient Egyptians used poppy seeds as a condiment, the Greeks gave them to their olympic athletes, and the Romans used them to decorate breads. An Indian legend relates that, not wanting to fall asleep, the Buddha cut off his eyelids and where they fell grew the first mauve opium poppies. During the 19th century, opium wars were fought between China and Britain to control trade in this narcotic.

In folklore, to prove the sincerity of a lover, a poppy petal was placed on the palm of one hand and then struck with the other; if the petal broke, he was true, but if it did not, he was false. In Oxfordshire, England, they say it is unlucky to bring poppies into the house. Red paper poppies are worn to honor the dead of this century's wars. This tradition stems from the bloody fields of the First World War, which were covered in red poppies, sometimes said to have sprung from the blood of fallen soldiers.

Below The large flowers of Papaver somniferum *can be white, pink, or purple. The seed pods contain tiny seeds, which are used as spice.*

ORIGINS AND CHARACTERISTICS

The poppy is from the *papaveraceae* family. It is native to Asia, where it is known as *ahiphenalm*, although it is now abundant in Europe. It is an erect annual with serrated, gray-green leaves, which grows about 4 foot high. Its large flowers have white, pink, or purple petals with dark basal spots, and a fat, flat-topped seed pod containing tiny seeds, which are used as a spice.

Opium, which is classified as poisonous, is the white latex in the walls of the seedhead, which is extracted before they are ripe. The variety of poppy that yields the best-quality opium is only grown in the Orient. European poppies give very little of the drug. A second pressing of the seeds produces a red oil suitable as artists' paint, which was used to color red ink.

Poppy seed

FLAVOR AND STORAGE

The seeds come in yellow, brown, and slate blue varieties, of which the blue is most common in the West. They are tiny and round, with a nutty, almost smoky, flavor. They are difficult to grind without a special mill, spice blender, or mortar and pestle. They should be stored in a sealed container in a cool, dry place.

PROPERTIES

Culinary Poppy seeds are rich in polyunsaturated fats and other nutrients, and are free from any narcotic content. They are widely used in Central European and Jewish cuisine. They can be added to cakes and pastries, and are sprinkled on sweet and savory biscuits, buns, and bread. Use a ¼ teaspoon in dips and spreads, soups, and salad dressings. A Czechoslovakian specialty is a light pastry filled with honey and poppy seeds. In India, poppy seeds are used to thicken and flavor curries. The oil extracted from the seeds can be used as a cooking oil.

Medicinal The alkaloids of the narcotic opium now supply important painkillers such as codeine, morphine, and heroin. It is included in preparations for sleeplessness and hyperactivity, and it helps the body absorb vitamin A. An infusion made from powdered poppyheads can be applied externally to give relief for sprains and bruises, whereas a flower compress helps to reduce dark circles around the eyes. Poppyheads have long been a rural remedy for toothache, neuralgia, and other nervous pains. Poppies were considered a potent remedy for the pangs of love, so were used in magic potions.

The Californian poppy, which is the state flower of California, has velvety, bright orange flowers and feathery leaves. It is used in flower remedies, similar to the famous Bach flower remedies, to assist emotional cleansing. Native Americans cooked the leaves on hot stones, and used them to treat toothache. Dried leaves and flowers are smoked to induce a mild euphoria with no known side effects. The Iceland poppy (*papaver nudicaule*) contains opiates, and is given as a painkiller.

Poppy Seed Swirls

Poppy seeds form the basis of the filling
in these crisp cookie swirls.

Makes about 48

Ingredients

½ cup walnut pieces, finely ground

½ cup poppy seeds

⅓ cup honey

½ tsp ground cinnamon

grated rind of 1 orange

6 tbsp unsalted butter, softened

½ cup superfine sugar

1 egg, lightly beaten

1 tsp vanilla extract

1½ cups all-purpose flour

Preparation

In a small bowl, combine the walnuts, poppy seeds, honey, cinnamon, orange rind, and 2 tbsp of the softened butter until mixture forms a paste. Set aside.

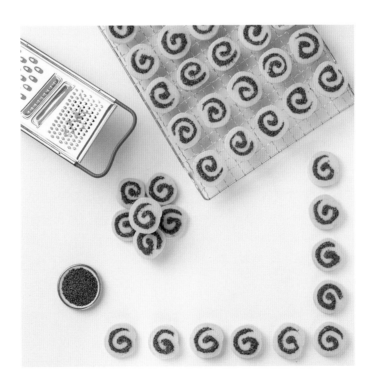

In a large bowl with electric mixer, beat the remaining butter and sugar until light and fluffy, 1–2 minutes. Beat in the egg and vanilla extract until well blended, then slowly beat in the flour until a soft dough forms. Refrigerate the dough until firm enough to handle, 15–20 minutes.

On a lightly floured sheet of waxed paper or non-stick baking parchment, roll out the dough to a 6 x 12-inch rectangle and spread with the poppy seed paste. Starting at one short side, roll up the dough jelly-roll fashion and wrap tightly. Refrigerate several hours or overnight until firm. (Dough can be refrigerated up to 5 days or frozen.)

Lightly grease 2 large non-stick baking sheets. Slice the dough roll crosswise into ¼-inch slices and place ½ inch apart on baking sheets. Bake at 375°F until golden, about 10 minutes. Remove the baking sheets to wire racks to cool slightly. Then using a metal pancake turner or palette knife, remove the cookies to wire racks to cool completely. Repeat with the remaining slices. Store in airtight containers.

Preparation time 20 minutes, plus chilling. Cooking time about 10 minutes per batch.

ALLSPICE
Pimento officinalis, P. dioica

IT IS OFTEN THOUGHT THAT ALLSPICE IS A MIXTURE OF CINNAMON, CLOVES, AND NUTMEG. ALTHOUGH THIS IS WHAT IT TASTES LIKE, IN FACT, ALLSPICE IS NOT A MIXTURE AT ALL. IT WAS ORIGINALLY USED BY NATIVE AMERICANS TO PRESERVE FISH AND MEAT.

ORIGINS AND CHARACTERISTICS

Allspice is the only popular spice never to be successfully cultivated away from its natural habitat, and is produced only in Central and South America, and the West Indies. It is a small "rotund" dark reddish-brown seed or berry that comes from a tropical tree of the myrtle family. This evergreen grows to 30 feet in height, and starts bearing fruit when about seven or eight years old. The berries grow in clusters surrounded by pointed leaves.

Most of the allspice berries or seeds come from Jamaica, so it is sometimes known as "Jamaican pepper." The trees are highly aromatic and the wood from the tree was once used to make walking sticks. Allspice has powerful preservative qualities. It was used extensively to preserve food on board ships during long journeys and still has a role in fish-packaging industries. Centuries before the Spanish arrived, the Mayan Indians of Central America used it to help preserve the bodies of their chiefs and nobles.

FLAVOR AND STORAGE

The French called allspice *quatre-épices* because it tastes like a mixture of cinnamon, cloves, ginger, and nutmeg. An English botanist gave it the name "allspice" after its mixed flavors. Although it is called Jamaican pepper, it is a mild, not a fiery spice. It is available as whole seeds or ground into a brown powder. It is better to buy the seeds and grind your own, as the powder soon loses its flavor and aroma. Store in a cool, dry place.

PROPERTIES

Culinary This spice is amazingly versatile, and is used to good effect in both sweet and piquant dishes. In England, it is particularly popular in Christmas recipes: Christmas cakes, Christmas puddings, mincemeat, and many other rich cakes and desserts. It is delicious with exotic sweets; try sprinkling a little allspice over tropical fruits, fresh, dried, or baked. Baked bananas with allspice works particularly well.

Allspice berries

Ground allspice

An appetizing use of this spice is to add it to stir-fried red cabbage with peanuts and apple, as well as to sauces, soups, and along with cooked meats. The preservative qualities of allspice are utilized in pickling fish, especially raw herrings. It is also used to flavor liqueurs, and makes a delicious addition to a cocktail of rum, lime juice, cinnamon, and brown sugar.

Medicinal and cosmetic Allspice is said to be good for rheumatism, headaches, flatulence, and all digestive problems. It used to be given to "highly strung young ladies" having an attack of "hysteria." The aromatic bark of the Californian allspice tree can be used to treat toothache. The leaves of *pimeruta racemosa* give bay oil, which, when mixed with rum, makes the famous bay rum aftershave. This concoction became popular with balding men, who claimed that applying it to their scalp helped their hair to grow. Allspice is also used to scent men's perfume.

Spiced Ham Casserole

This colorful ham casserole is flavored with fruits.

Serves 4–6

Preparation time 15 minutes. Cooking time 1 hour 20 minutes.

Ingredients

1½ lb smoked ham, diced

2 tbsp vegetable oil

1 medium onion, finely chopped

2 tbsp all-purpose flour

1¼ cups medium/dry cider

½ tsp allspice

freshly ground black pepper

1 medium zucchini, sliced

1 small green eating apple, cored and sliced

1 peach, peeled and sliced

1 orange, peeled and sectioned

Preparation

Cut the ham into bite-sized pieces. Place in a pan of cold water, bring to a boil and discard liquid. Repeat and drain.

Heat the oil in a large saucepan, add the onion and cook gently, without browning, until softened. Stir in the flour, gradually add the cider and bring to a boil, stirring. Add the allspice and pepper. Cover and cook gently for 1 hour.

Add the zucchini, apple, peach, and orange, and continue cooking for a further 20 minutes before serving.

ANISEED
Pimpinella anisum

ANISEED, ALSO SOMETIMES KNOWN AS SWEET CUMIN, IS USED TO FLAVOR SPIRITS SUCH AS PERNOD AND OUZO. IT ALSO MAKES A REFRESHING TEA, WHEN SWEETENED WITH HONEY. BEEKEEPERS MAKE A LIGHT HONEY FROM THE FLOWER'S NECTAR. IT IS ONE OF THE OLDEST CULTIVATED SPICES.

Above *The flowers of* Pimpinella anisum *grow in clusters, called umbels.*

Dutch aniseed

ORIGINS AND CHARACTERISTICS

Aniseed is native to Egypt and the East Mediterranean, but is now grown in many countries. The anis plant grows about 20 inches high. Its aromatic leaves are rounded and serrated around the edges at the base of the plant, and get narrower as they grow up the stem. The flowers grow in clusters, called umbels, and the aromatic fruit are curved in shape.

Its botanical cousin, the Japanese anis (*Illicium anusattum*), grows to 60 feet in height, and has a poisonous cardamom-scented fruit. The Japanese treat it with great reverence, and burn the bark as incense. These trees are often found planted near Buddhist temples and monasteries.

FLAVOR AND STORAGE

Aniseed is famous for its strong licorice flavor, giving the characteristic tang to aniseed balls. It also has a marked aroma. It is best bought as whole seeds, which, although they have a short shelf life, retain their flavor longer than ground powder. Store in an airtight container away from sunlight.

PROPERTIES

Culinary The whole or crushed seeds enhance relishes, tomato soups, stews, and curries, especially if the seeds are roasted. They also work well with desserts. The flowers can be added to fruit salads, the young leaves make a splendid garnish, and the root can be used in stews and sweet soups.

Medicinal and cosmetic Aniseed quells nausea and aids digestion, and small amounts are used in toothpastes, mouthwashes, and cough mixtures. The seeds used to be taken in the form of sugared comfits as a digestive. Aniseed is also said to be an aphrodisiac, stimulating the libido.

PEPPER
Piper nigrum

PEPPER IS CALLED "THE KING OF SPICES," AND HAS BEEN AN IMPORTANT SPICE FOR OVER 400 YEARS. IN TIMES PAST, PEPPERCORNS WERE HIGHLY VALUED. IN 408 AD, THE RANSOM DEMANDED BY THE VISIGOTHS FOR NOT SACKING THE CITY OF ROME WAS GOLD, SILVER, AND 3,000 POUNDS OF PEPPERCORNS. THE VENERABLE BEDE, THE 9TH-CENTURY ENGLISH HISTORIAN AND THEOLOGIAN, TREASURED PEPPER AMONG HIS FEW POSSESSIONS WHICH HE LEFT HIS FELLOW PRIESTS AFTER HIS DEATH. GROCERS WERE ORIGINALLY KNOWN AS PEPPERERS. PEPPERCORNS WERE INCLUDED IN A BRIDE'S DOWRY AND WERE OFTEN USED AS A FORM OF CURRENCY. RENT WAS OFTEN PAID IN PEPPER, HENCE THE TERM "PEPPERCORN RENT." IT WAS THE SEARCH FOR PEPPER THAT SENT EXPLORERS AROUND THE WORLD AND LED TO THE DISCOVERY OF AMERICA.

Below *Peppercorns grow on a perennial vine,* Piper nigrum, *that reaches up to 13 feet in height.*

ORIGINS AND CHARACTERISTICS

Pepper's name comes from the Sanskrit *pippali nigrum*, which means "black spice." Peppercorns grow on a perennial vine that reaches up to 13 feet in height; it has a thick stem, white flowering spikes, and broad, dark green leaves with parallel veins running down each leaf. The green to dark red fruit grows in long, catkin-like groups of berries. The plant starts to bear berries from between two to five years, and can continue bearing fruit for about 40 years. It is native to the Malabar coast of southwest India, but it is now also cultivated in Indonesia, Thailand, Malaysia, and Brazil.

The black, green, and red peppercorns are all made from the berries picked at different stages of their growth and then processed differently. For black peppercorns, the unripe green fruit is dried with its outer skin intact: either sun dried or immersed in boiling water before being dried in kilns, which turns them into wrinkled, black peppercorns. For white peppercorns, the berries are picked ripe, when they are red, soaked so that the outer skin is easily removed by rubbing, washing, and trampling to leave the smooth, light-colored core, which is then sun dried. Green peppercorns are berries that are picked unripe, dried artificially to retain their color, then pickled and preserved either by bottling or canning.

There are about 50 different varieties of peppercorn plants, including *piper sarmentosum*, an herbaceous plant whose leaves are eaten raw and which has medicinal qualities; *piper betle*, which has heart-shaped, aromatic leaves; and *piper longum*, which has densely arranged spikes of fruit that are gathered green and dried to produce a spice that is sweeter than black pepper, and is used mainly in Asian cooking.

FLAVOR AND STORAGE

Peppercorns have a pungent, woody aroma and a hot, biting taste. They are best ground as required from a pepper mill since ground pepper soon loses its flavor, whereas peppercorns can last for years. White pepper is hot, but milder than black pepper and not so aromatic.

Green peppercorns have a pleasantly mild and aromatic flavor, and can be mashed to a paste for use in butter and sauces. They are preserved in brine or vinegar. The essential oil from peppercorns gives commercial foods a peppery flavor without the pungency.

Different peppers can be mixed in a pepper mill to give a combination of these spices. Mignonette pepper is a mixture of white and black peppercorns. In India, they often prefer a mix of ground spices, instead of just salt and pepper, as condiments on the dining table. Try filling a saltcellar with a combination of coarse salt, black peppercorns, and roasted cumin seeds—about one tablespoonful of each, all freshly grated. If this mixture is kept in an airtight container it will stay reasonably fresh for a couple of weeks.

PROPERTIES

Culinary Pepper is the only spice that is used to flavor food before, during, and after cooking. Whole or cracked peppercorns can be added to peppered steak, soups, casseroles, and most non-sweet dishes. They are good added to vinaigrette, and combine wonderfully with soft cheeses to make delicacies such as *boursin au poivre*, a soft cheese covered in coarse pepper. They are important in pickling and in spicy vinegars, and can even be added to strawberries along with a sprinkling of balsamic vinegar.

Green peppers contribute a pungency that is less sharp than black pepper. Some say that white pepper should be used with pale-colored food, and black with dark food.

Medicinal and cosmetic The alkaloid piperine found in pepper stimulates the saliva and gastric juices, killing bacteria, improving the appetite, aiding digestion, and reducing flatulence and nausea. It is also reputedly good for constipation, rheumatism, diarrhea, colic, and headaches. Included in a massage oil, it helps tone muscles. *Piper longum* root is used as an expectorant to help release phlegm, while *piper betle* leaves are chewed with betel-nuts to promote general wellbeing. Pepper is also an insecticide, and will keep flies away and deter moths if scattered over clothes or fabrics. It is used for its aroma to add spicy overtones to perfumes.

Classic French Vinaigrette

Other flavored oils can be substituted.

Makes about 1 cup

Preparation time 5 minutes.

Ingredients

½ tsp salt

⅛ tsp freshly ground black pepper

¼ cup vinegar or lemon juice

¼–½ tsp Dijon-style mustard

¾ cup walnut or olive oil

Preparation

Whisk together the salt, pepper, vinegar or lemon juice, mustard, and walnut or olive oil in a nonreactive medium bowl. The dressing will keep for about 3 days in the refrigerator.

Black and red pepper

Black peppercorns

Ground white pepper

Coarse ground black pepper

Tropical mixed peppercorns

Ground black pepper

Pomegranate fruit

POMEGRANATE
Punica granatum

THE POMEGRANATE IS AN ANCIENT SYMBOL OF FERTILITY, AND ITS VERMILION FLOWER IS THE EMBLEM OF SPAIN. THE FRUIT, BARK, AND RIND YIELD FABRIC DYES.

ORIGINS AND CHARACTERISTICS

Pomegranate is a shiny fruit the size of an orange, colloquially known as "Apple of Carthage." It grows on a small deciduous tree of the *punicaceae* family that in dry conditions can reach 20 feet in height. Pomegranate trees sometimes have spiny branches, and are covered in beautifully colored foliage in spring and fall, and picturesque vermilion, fragrant flowers in summer. The perfumed flowers have crinkly, paper-like petals and fleshy sepals. The ripe fruit has a smooth, tough, yellow-red-orange rind; the inside is crimson, with a juicy, edible pulp with pale seeds. Pomegranates are indigenous to southwest Asia, but now grow in many tropical and subtropical environments.

FLAVOR AND STORAGE

Anardana is a sour Indian condiment made from the dried seeds with their aril, the fleshy appendage found on some seeds. The sour pulp is boiled to make pomegranate syrup. The fruit will last in the refrigerator for a few days, but the dried seeds should be kept in an airtight jar.

PROPERTIES

Culinary Pomegranate fruits can be eaten raw as a fruit, sucked into the mouth for the juice and the bits discarded. Commercially, the juice is extracted mechanically, and is used to make grenadine, a flavoring for cocktails, sherbets, and relishes.

Pomegranate syrup is used in Middle Eastern cooking. Indian *anardana* is a souring agent in curries, chutneys, pulse dishes, is used as a filling for pastries and bread, and is sprinkled on foods such as hummus, curries, and paratha bread. In the Middle East, Turkey and Iran, raw seeds are often used as a garnish.

Medicinal Pomegranate rind is reputedly helpful in the treatment of dysentery, and the root bark to combat tapeworm.

Above *The perfumed flowers of the pomegranate tree,* Punica granatum, *have crinkly, paper-like petals.*

Right *Pomegranate seeds.*

QUASSIA
Quassia amara

THIS HEALING SPICE WAS NAMED AFTER A GUYANAN SLAVE CALLED
QUASSI, WHO FIRST SHOWED EUROPEANS ITS FEVER-TREATING QUALITIES.

ORIGINS AND CHARACTERISTICS

Quassia is also known as bitterwood. It comes
from a tropical South American tree of the *simaroubacae* family, which grows about 10 feet high and looks like an
ash tree. Its leaves emerge red, then mature to green with an extended point. They grow in opposite pairs and
have winged leaf-stalks flushed with purple. It has racemes of red flowers with white interiors, and berries that
ripen to purple-black. Quassia is a bitter compound extracted from the wood and bark.

FLAVOR AND STORAGE

Quassia chips have an intense bitter flavor, but
no aroma. They are best stored in a dry, airtight container away from light.

PROPERTIES

Culinary At one time brewers used chips of
quassia wood instead of hops to flavor beer. Added to water or alcohol, these produce an extremely bitter yellow
liquid traditionally drunk in the spring to clear the digestive system after a winter of stodgy salted food.

Medicinal The bitter bark is used in an alcoholic tonic drink.
In the past, a cup made of quassia wood and filled with water was left overnight to produce a bitter drink said to be good for
stimulating gastric juices and strengthening the appetite. If you make this tea for yourself, don't forget to strain the chips before
you drink it. The stem chips are reputedly useful in the treatment of malaria, rheumatism, fevers, dyspepsia, and are taken to
expel worms. It is also said to help cure alcoholism, and is used as an infusion to make a shampoo for dandruff.

Quassia is employed as a poison in fly papers, and has also
be found to be useful as an insecticide.

Above Quassia amara *tree*.

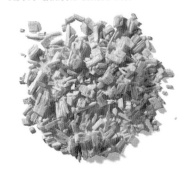

Quassia chips

Above Rhus coriaria *is a deciduous shrub from the* anacardiacea *family.*

Below *Sumac.*

SUMAC
Rhus coriaria

ALTHOUGH NOT WIDELY KNOWN IN THE WEST, SUMAC WAS USED AS A SPICE BY THE ROMANS BEFORE THE INTRODUCTION OF LEMONS, TO ADD AN ASTRINGENT QUALITY TO PIQUANT DISHES. THEY ALSO USED the flowers to color rice.

ORIGINS AND CHARACTERISTICS

Sumac is a deciduous shrub from the *anacardiacea* family which thrives in dry, open scrubland in the Mediterranean and North America. It is only the Mediterranean variety, however, whose seeds yield a spice, as the others are poisonous. It is mainly cultivated in Turkey and Lebanon.

Sumac grows about 33 feet high, with a long stem and small leaves that turn vermilion in the fall. It produces a cluster of brick-red, acid-flavored berries, containing brown, spicy seeds, both used as spices. Smooth sumac (*rhus glabra*), also called the vinegar tree, is a North American variety that grows to 10 feet.

FLAVOR AND STORAGE

Sumac gives a sharp, fruity flavor similar to lemon, but less harsh; it adds a subtle astringent taste to foods. The fresh berries and seeds must be used fairly quickly, though it is also available dried and powdered. The powder quickly loses its flavor, so it is best to grind your own, as the dried seeds and berries will keep for months. All sumac should be stored in an airtight jar out of direct sunlight.

PROPERTIES

Culinary Sumac is used as a souring agent in Middle Eastern dishes such as rice, vegetables, stews, pulses, dips, and sauces. The powdered berries are used to flavor meat and fish, while juice from the soaked seeds and dried berries is added to salad dressings, yogurt, sauces, and marinades. Sicilian sumac produces the best-flavored berries, which when soaked give a fruity-sour culinary juice much preferred by Middle Eastern cooks.

Medicinal The mountain sumac (*rhus copallina*) is a deciduous tree with red berries, whose roots are said to be helpful in the treatment of dysentery.

SESAME
Sesamum indicum

SESAME WAS BELIEVED TO HAVE MAGICAL POWERS, HENCE THE FAMOUS CALL OF "OPEN SESAME" FROM THE FOLKTALE ALI BABA AND THE FORTY THIEVES. THIS BELIEF PROBABLY STEMMED FROM THE STARTLING TENDENCY OF THE SEEDPODS TO BURST OPEN SUDDENLY WITH A SHARP POP. AFRICAN SLAVES BROUGHT SESAME TO AMERICA BECAUSE THEY THOUGHT IT WAS A GOOD-LUCK CHARM, WHILE IN ARABIA IT WAS USED AS AN APHRODISIAC. CLEOPATRA ALSO USED SESAME OIL AS A SKIN MOISTURIZER.

ORIGINS AND CHARACTERISTICS

Sesame probably originated in Asia or East Africa, but has now spread throughout the tropics, particularly being grown in Africa, Indonesia, India, and Afghanistan. It is also known as *benne*, an African name for sesame. The seeds that give this spice come from a plant of the *pedaliaceae* family—an annual that grows between 2–9 feet tall, with a single, erect stem, oval leaves, and white or pink flowers. Its long seed capsules burst open when they are dry, scattering the seeds and making harvesting very labor-intensive. In 1943, a nonscattering mutant was discovered, allowing mechanical harvesting. The pressed and refined oil from the seed is popular in Chinese cooking.

Above Sesamum indicum *grows between 2–9 feet tall with a single, erect stem.*

FLAVOR AND STORAGE

Sesame seeds smell and taste like toasted nuts. They can be bought as white polished and hulled seeds, buff-colored unhulled seeds, and black unhulled seeds. They should be stored in an airtight container kept in a cool, dry place and then ground, if desired, when needed. The oil is extremely stable.

Below Sesame seed.

PROPERTIES

Culinary Sesame seeds are very nutritious. Vegetarians eat a lot of sesame seeds, because they contain so much protein and make a pleasant change from nuts. Their seeds' nutty flavor can be enhanced by dry roasting. They make an excellent addition to stir-fries or noodles, and are delicious when gently fried in butter and tossed over a green salad or whipped into mashed potatoes or avocado. As well as spicy dishes, they can be sprinkled on bread, pastries, cookies,and cakes. Sesame seed honey bars can be bought as confectionery.

In the Middle East, sesame seeds are ground to make *halvah*, as well as *tahini* paste, which is served with garlic or lemon and used as a flavoring for hummus. Ground seeds are used in Indian cuisine, whole lightly roasted seeds in some Chinese dishes, and black sesame seeds are extensively used in Japanese cooking.

Golden sesame oil from unroasted seeds and dark sesame oil from roasted seeds are both used in cooking, mainly for Oriental dishes. The oil has a unique taste that makes it delicious in salad dressings, and it is a common ingredient of margarine.

Medicinal In China, the seeds and oil are used for treating weak kidneys, liver complaints, coughs, rheumatism, paralysis, and incontinence. A poultice of the seeds, ground and mixed with hot water, has been used to treat bleeding hemorrhoids. The oil is used in suntan lotion, ointments, and laxatives.

Sesame Garbanzo Beans with Chicken

This recipe transforms leftover cooked chicken into a stylish meal.

Serves 4

Preparation time 10–15 minutes. Cooking time 10–15 minutes.

Ingredients

1 lettuce heart, shredded
2-inch piece cucumber, peeled and diced
1 bunch radishes, sliced
2 tbsp roasted sesame seeds
4 tbsp olive oil
2 x 15 oz cans garbanzo beans, drained
1 lb cooked chicken, diced
6 tbsp *tahini*
4 tbsp snipped chives
2 tbsp chopped fresh parsley
salt and freshly ground black pepper
2 avocados, halved, pitted, peeled, and cut in chunks
½ cup black olives, halved
1 lemon, cut into wedges

Preparation

Mix the lettuce, cucumber, radishes, and sesame seeds, then arrange this salad around the edge of four serving plates or one large dish.

Heat the oil, then stir fry the garbanzo beans and chicken for about 5 minutes, or until the chicken is thoroughly heated. Stir in the *tahini* until it combines with the oil to coat the ingredients in a creamy dressing. Add the herbs, seasoning, and avocados, then stir the black olives into the mixture.

Divide the chicken mixture between the serving plates and garnish with lemon wedges. The lemon juice should be squeezed over the chicken mixture and salad.

TAMARIND
Tamarindus indica

MUSLIMS PREPARE A SPECIAL TAMARIND DRINK DURING THE HOLY MONTH OF RAMADAN. IT IS ALSO THE BASE FOR SHERBETS AND OTHER LONG COOL DRINKS.

ORIGINS AND CHARACTERISTICS

Tamarind, sometimes known as "Indian date," comes from an evergreen tree of the *leguminosae* family that can reach nearly 80 feet. It has arching branches of attractive foliage, and hanging racemes of cream flowers with rose- or yellow-colored veins. The fruit is about 2–8 inches long. When ripe, these pods contain a sour pulp rich in vitamins and minerals; it is this pulp around the shiny dark seeds that is used as a spice. Tamarind is probably native to Africa, but now grows also in India, Southeast Asia, and the West Indies.

FLAVOR AND STORAGE

Tamarind has a fruity, sour taste. Generally the pods are dried, peeled and seeded, and packed into cellophane-wrapped bricks that are sold in ethnic groceries. Make sure the brick you buy is pliable; the harder it is, the more difficult it is to release its pulp. When bought dried, it must be soaked first in hot water for ten minutes, then squeezed. The pod and seeds are discarded and the liquid is used. The dried blocks can be stored in an airtight tin or indefinitely in a refrigerator, but the liquid is best freshly prepared.

PROPERTIES

Culinary Tamarind is used much like lemon or as a substitute for vinegar. It adds a distinctive cooling quality to curries, chutneys, satays, and Caribbean sweetmeats. In Thailand, the flowers and leaves are used for flavoring, while in India the seed pectin is used in jam-making. This spice is used in commercial products such as Angostura bitters and Worcestershire sauce.

Medicinal and cosmetic Tamarind is a mild laxative. The bark is said to be good for asthma, a seed or leaf paste for boils, the flowers for high blood pressure. The rich pulp is used in Chinese medicine. Red and yellow dyes are derived from the tree's astringent leaves.

Clockwise from top left *Tamarind seed; tamarind pods; Tamarindus indica, flower and fruit; dried ground tamarind; tamarind block.*

FENUGREEK
Trigonella foenum-graecum

LEAVE A HEAPED TABLESPOON OF FENUGREEK SEEDS JUST COVERED WITH BOILING WATER IN A TEAPOT OVERNIGHT. IN THE MORNING, ADD FRESH BOILING WATER, ALLOW A FEW MINUTES TO INFUSE, AND ADD LEMON JUICE AND HONEY TO PRODUCE AN ENJOYABLE AND CLEANSING MORNING DRINK.

Top *Fenugreek seed.*

Above *Dried fenugreek leaves.*

Below Trigonella foenum-graecum.

Top right *Ground fenugreek.*

ORIGINS AND CHARACTERISTICS

Fenugreek is of the *leguminosae* family, a short, upright plant with oval leaves that grow in threes and yellow-white flowers. Its narrow, curved pods hold between 10–20 small, three-sided, yellow seeds. These aromatic seeds contain vitamins, iron, and minerals, and yield a yellow dye.

This spice is indigenous to east Mediterranean countries, and was used by the Greeks as cattle fodder, hence the colloquial name "Greek hay." It is also cultivated in India.

FLAVOR AND STORAGE

The entire plant has a strong, sweet aroma and a pleasantly bitter taste a bit like burnt sugar. The dried leaves smell of new-mown hay. The mature leaves have the strongest bitter taste. Ground fenugreek has a warm, yellowish-brown color with a strong curry-like taste. It is best stored in an airtight glass container.

PROPERTIES

Culinary The roasted seeds are used to flavor chutneys and curries, and are soaked and eaten like beans in parts of Africa; they can also be added to Egyptian and Ethiopian breads. Sprouted seeds make an interesting addition to salads. Ground seeds give a slightly maple flavor to *halvah*, a Turkish sweetmeat made with sesame and honey. The clover-like leaves are eaten in India as a leaf vegetable.

Medicinal Fenugreek is an ingredient of many modern medicines. It reduces blood cholesterol and urine sugar, so is good for diabetes. Made into a paste and spread all over the body, it is said to be revitalizing and to reduce fevers. Poultices made with fenugreek are excellent for wounds, and it makes a good gargle for sore throats and mouth ulcers. Fenugreek is considered an aphrodisiac and a hair-growing stimulant.

VANILLA
Vanilla planifolia

VANILLA GETS ITS NAME FROM THE SPANISH VANILLA, A DIMINUTIVE OF VAINA, MEANING "SHEATH." THE AZTEC EMPEROR REGULARLY DRANK A CONCOCTION MADE FROM POWDERED COCOA BEANS AND GROUND CORN FLAVORED WITH VANILLA BEANS AND HONEY. THE SPANISH TOOK VANILLA HOME WITH THEM TO EUROPE, WHERE IT BECAME VERY POPULAR AS A FLAVORING IN THE CHOCOLATE INDUSTRY.

ORIGINS AND CHARACTERISTICS

Vanilla beans are taken from a tropical climbing orchid with a long, fleshy stem that grows upward to a height of 50 feet, using aerial roots that attach themselves to trees as well as growing into the soil. It flourishes in sandy soil shaded from direct sun. Its leaves are bright green, pointed, about 3 inches wide, and anything between 4–9 inches long. The waxy, fragrant, pale green flowers only bloom for a single day, and open a few at a time during a two-month season. In Mexico, they are naturally pollinated by bees and hummingbirds, but in other countries they must be hand-pollinated. The vines start bearing fruit in their third year. The vanilla beans are picked when yellow, unripe, and scentless, and are cured by a five-month course of repeated sweating and drying, during which they turn a deep brown.

Vanilla is a native to Mexico, and North and South America. There is also a Tahitian variety called *vanilla tabitensis*. For centuries Mexico was the main producer, because it was not until 1836 that the Belgian botanist Charles Morren realized this plant needed to be hand-pollinated. It is now chiefly grown in the Malagasy Republic, the Comoro islands, Mauritius, Java, Mexico, and Uganda.

FLAVOR AND STORAGE

Vanilla beans should be kept in the package until opened, then stored in a jar or buried in sugar. Quality beans are plump and supple. If your beans develop a whitish tinge, don't worry: it is just the natural sugars crystallizing on the surface. When needed, cut about 2 inches from a bean and slit down the middle to release the flavor. After use, it should be rinsed and dried so that it can be used a further two or three times.

The bean may be ground, or soaked or boiled in a liquid such as milk, in order to extract the flavor. The liquid may be used as well as the vanilla, as it will have absorbed lots of flavor. Vanilla essence is obtained by crushing the dried beans, extracting the oil with alcohol, and then sweetening with syrup.

Above *The waxy, fragrant flowers of* Vanilla planifolia *bloom for one day only.*

PROPERTIES

Culinary Vanilla is used to flavor candy, ice cream, chocolate, cakes, biscuits, custards, and dessert sauces. If the cut pieces are stored in a small jar of sugar, the sugar will absorb a gorgeous vanilla flavor. "Vanilla flavor" on commercial food labels does not necessarily mean vanilla has been included, but could mean artificial flavor and color, possibly eugenol extracted from oil of cloves.

Medicinal Vanilla is a digestive stimulant, but too much can cause inflammation. It is also reputedly an antidote to some poisons, affects the nervous system, and was believed to be a tonic for the brain. In early times it was held to be a stimulant and an aphrodisiac.

Real Vanilla Butter Cookies

These cookies are a Danish specialty. They use real vanilla seeds from a bean, but you can use a good-quality vanilla extract, although they won't be quite as authentic.

Makes about 24

Preparation time 20 minutes. Cooking time 8–10 minutes.

Ingredients

2 cups less 2 tbsp all-purpose flour

2 tbsp cornstarch

5 tbsp sugar

⅓ cup blanched almonds, finely chopped

½ vanilla bean or 1 tsp vanilla extract

1 cup unsalted butter, cut into small pieces

1 egg, separated

sugar for sprinkling

confectioners' sugar for dusting

Preparation

Lightly grease 2 large baking sheets. Into a large bowl, sift together the flour and cornstarch; stir in the sugar and almonds.

Using a sharp knife, split the vanilla bean and scrape out the seeds. Add to the flour mixture and mix well. (If using vanilla extract, mix with the egg yolk and add later.)

Using a pastry blender or electric mixer on slow speed, rub the butter into the flour until fine crumbs form. In a small bowl, beat the egg yolk (and vanilla extract, if using). Add to the flour-butter mixture and knead until soft but firm dough forms. (If the dough is very sticky, sprinkle over a little more flour.)

Spoon the dough into a large pastry bag fitted with a large plain tip, and pipe 2-inch "doughnut" shapes 1½ inches apart on the baking sheets. In a small bowl, beat the egg white until foamy, and brush each ring. Sprinkle with sugar.

Bake at 400°F until lightly golden and set, 8–10 minutes.

Remove the baking sheets to wire racks to cool slightly. Then, using a metal pancake turner, remove the cookies to wire racks to cool completely. Dust with confectioners' sugar. Store in airtight containers.

Vanilla pods

WASABI
Wasabia japonica

WASABI COMES FROM A JAPANESE PLANT KNOWN AS MOUNTAIN HOLLYHOCK. IT GROWS WILD, PREFERING A COASTAL ENVIRONMENT OR COOL MOUNTAIN STREAMS. IT IS SOMETIMES CALLED JAPANESE HORSERADISH, AND IS ALMOST EXCLUSIVELY USED IN JAPANESE CUISINE.

ORIGINS AND CHARACTERISTICS

Wasabi is part of the *cruciferae* family and grows about 16 inches high. It has crinkled, shiny, heart-shaped leaves and clusters of small, white flowers, with four petals to each flower. The stalks are green or purple. It produces a long, narrow seed pod, and has a thick rhizome that is used as a spice. Wasabi takes two years to mature, starting out pale when young, then developing to a rich reddish-purple.

FLAVOR AND STORAGE

The Japanese love the bright color and strong, fiery, clean flavor of wasabi. It is available as a dried powder or pale green paste. The powder will keep its aroma and flavor longer than the paste, so it is preferable to buy the former and mix it into a paste yourself by adding water and leaving it to infuse before use. The powder should be kept in an airtight container. The paste should be stored in the refrigerator since it loses its flavor quickly.

The grated rhizome soon loses its flavor, and must be used as fresh as possible. It is seldom found outside Japan, although it may be available in some Oriental grocery shops.

PROPERTIES

Culinary Wasabi is perfect for and unique to Japanese cuisine, and is served with plates of *sashimi*, mixed to taste with a soy dipping sauce, and with *sushi*, *soba*, and *tofu*, as well as mixed with *shoyu* (Japanese soy sauce). It is the peeled and grated rhizome that is most commonly used as a spice, but the leaves and stalks are also sometimes included in cooking.

Medicinal Wasabi is said to kill parasites that may be present in raw fish, a popular Japanese dish.

Wasabi powder

FAGARA (SICHUAN PEPPER)
Zanthoxylum piperitum

Below Leaves and fruit of
Zanthoxylum piperitum *in*
the full.

FAGARA IS USED IN CHINESE-STYLE SALT AND PEPPER, AND IS
VITAL TO THE CHARACTERISTIC TASTE OF MUCH CHINESE FOOD.

ORIGINS AND CHARACTERISTICS

Indigenous to China and Japan, fagara is from the *rutaceae*
family, and falls somewhere between a tree and a shrub, having as it does both male and female plants. It grows to around 22
feet high, and has very aromatic leaves that are sold in bundles. They grow in pairs, and are followed farther down the stem by
paired, sharp, splinter-type thorns. This plant flowers into small, yellow-green blossoms in spring, and develops spicy, reddish-
brown berries in the fall.

FLAVOR AND STORAGE

The Chinese like the spicy, woody flavor of the berries dried
without their bitter black seeds, and use them as a condiment. The berries without their seeds are commonly called Sichuan
pepper. The Japanese use the powdered berries, which they call Sancho pepper. They also preserve the flower buds in soy sauce
and rice wine. Fagara can be stored in a dry, airtight container, although the seeds will last well in a pepper grinder.

PROPERTIES

Culinary The Japanese sprinkle fagara on food and use the
young leaves to garnish soups, while the young shoots are used with the soybean paste *miso*. Fagara is an ingredient in the
Japanese seven-spice mixture called *shichimi*, and in the classic spice combination, the Chinese five-spice mixture. It is vital to the
characteristic taste of Sichuan dishes.

Fagar peppercorns are also used in Chinese-style salt and
pepper. Combine 4 tablespoons coarse salt with 1½ tablespoons Sichuan peppercorns, and heat in a small cast-iron pan over
medium-low heat. Stir for 5 minutes, or until the salt turns darker and the pepper gives off a wonderful aroma, then grind the
mixture in a coffee grinder.

Below The dried berries, without the
bitter seeds.

GINGER
Zingiber officinale

GINGER WAS ONE OF THE FIRST SPICES TO ARRIVE IN THE WEST FROM CHINA. THE CHINESE SAGE CONFUCIUS MENTIONS IT IN THE 5TH CENTURY BC, AND IT WAS A FAVORITE AMONG THE ROMANS, RIVALED ONLY BY PEPPER IN ITS POPULARITY. IN THE 5TH CENTURY, IT WAS GROWN IN POTS ON BOARD SHIP TO PREVENT SEAFARERS SUFFERING FROM THE DEADLY SCURVY. ENGLAND'S HENRY VIII WAS A GINGER ADDICT, AND WAS CONVINCED THIS SPICE WAS A BASIC INGREDIENT IN ANY CONCOCTION USED TO FIGHT THE PLAGUE. HIS DAUGHTER, ELIZABETH I, SHARED HIS ENTHUSIASM, AND HAD HER COOK MAKE GINGERBREAD IN THE LIKENESS OF HER COURTIERS—THE ORIGINAL GINGERBREAD MEN.

ORIGINS AND CHARACTERISTICS

Ginger is a root of a perennial from Southeast Asia. Its generic name means "shaped like a horn" because it sometimes resembles deer's antlers; fresh ginger roots are often also referred to as "hands," because of their shape. There are about a dozen different varieties of ginger, both wild and cultivated. The plant can grow to about 3 feet, and has long leaves that grow in vertical lines alternately down the stem. Its flowers can be yellow, green, or purple, depending on the variety, and grow in clusters.

The Spanish introduced ginger to Chile and Mexico, and before long it was grown voraciously all over the Caribbean to be exported back to Spain. It now grows in the West Indies, Hawaii, Africa and Northern Australia. China and India are the biggest producers.

Above *The spice comes from the root of the perennial* Zingiber officinale.

Left *Fresh rhizome.*

Dried root ginger

Ground ginger

Chinese ground ginger

Cochin ginger

FLAVOR AND STORAGE

Ginger is a knobbly rhizome with a sweet aroma and hot, pungent taste. It can be purchased as a root, a powder, or as a stem of ginger in syrup. When buying this spice, always look for a root with a smooth skin; if it is wrinkled, it is drying out and will be hard and woody inside. Fresh ginger can be kept for short periods in an airy container alongside your garlic. If you use it infrequently, however, it is best to wrap it in newspaper and keep it in the refrigerator. For longer periods of storage, it can also be peeled, chopped into small pieces, and placed in a glass screwtop jar containing enough brandy or sherry to cover the root completely. This method preserves it for months, and when it is needed, you can use the liquid rather than the root—a delicious addition to most recipes that require ginger. After use, top up the jar with a little more alcohol as necessary. A way of storing this spice which gives you a perpetual supply of ginger is to bury it in sand; it can be used as required, but will continue to grow in the meantime.

Ginger makes a tasty paste, especially if mixed with garlic. For this you will need to peel the ginger, which is much easier if you have soaked it overnight first. Chop the root into small pieces and grind with peeled garlic and a minimum of water into a fine paste, mixing in a pinch of salt. Fine-toothed ginger/horseradish graters are particularly efficient at getting rid of the tough fibers, leaving only the pulp. If you are using a food processor, it is best to start the machine first, with the metal blades in place, adding the ginger and garlic, and last of all the water. Add some salt to the paste, and mix well. The paste can be stored in a plastic bag kept in a sealed container, and will remain usable for about a month, whether in or out of the refrigerator. It has a strong odor, however, and is best not stored alongside other foods.

PROPERTIES

Culinary Ginger can be used in sweet dishes such as ice creams, desserts, ginger cookies and cakes, or in piquant dishes such as hot curries and stir fries. Fresh ginger is widely used in Oriental cooking. Whole dried roots have a powerful flavor ideal for pickling and chutneys, and also make hot and cold drinks like ginger beer and ginger tea. In the past, innkeepers used to sprinkle it on porter, a dark brown bitter brewed from charred malt, and then stir it with a red hot poker, before giving it to guests that had just got off the stagecoach on a winter's night.

Medicinal Ginger has a warming effect on the stomach, which soothes digestion. It induces sweating and so is said to be useful as an antidote to poison, as well as for colds, flu, cramps, and paralyzed limbs. It is also regarded as a heart strengthener, and is good for liver complaints, flatulence, anaemia, piles, and jaundice. Mixed with senna leaves, it is an excellent laxative. Ginger is also commonly regarded as an aphrodisiac, while a teaspoon of ginger in warm water is said to guard against travel sickness. Ginger tea helps in menstruation and with the pains of childbirth.

Gingerbread Shapes

This rich, spicy dough can be cut into anything you want: boys, girls, santas and reindeer, or hearts and flowers.

Makes about 24

Preparation time 25 minutes, plus chilling and drying.

Cooking time 10–12 minutes per batch.

Ingredients

3½ cups all-purpose flour

1 tsp salt

1 tsp baking powder

1½ tsp ground ginger

1½ tsp ground cinnamon

1½ tsp allspice

1 tsp ground cloves

½ tsp finely ground white pepper

1 cup (2 sticks) unsalted butter or margarine, softened

⅔ cup packed dark brown sugar

½ cup light molasses

1 egg

Royal Icing

2½ cups confectioners' sugar

¼ tsp cream of tartar

2 egg whites

food coloring (optional)

1 tbsp lemon juice or rum

Preparation

Into a large bowl, sift together the flour, salt, baking powder, ginger, cinnamon, allspice, cloves, and pepper; set aside.
In a large bowl with an electric mixer, beat the butter or margarine and brown sugar until light and fluffy, 1–2 minutes.

Beat in the molasses and egg until well blended. On low speed, beat in the flour mixture until a soft dough forms.
Scrape the dough into a piece of plastic wrap or waxed paper and, using the wrap or paper as a guide, shape into a flat disk. Wrap tightly, and refrigerate several hours or overnight until firm enough to roll. (Dough can be made up to 2 days ahead.) Lightly grease 2 large baking sheets. On a lightly floured surface, using a floured rolling pin, roll out half the dough ¼ inch thick (keep remaining dough refrigerated). With a floured 4-inch gingerbread boy or girl cutter, cut out as many cookies as possible. Arrange the cookies 1 inch apart on a baking sheet, because they will expand during cooking.

Bake at 350°F until edges are lightly browned, 10–12 minutes. Remove the baking sheets to wire racks to cool slightly. Then, using a metal pancake turner or palette knife, remove the cookies to wire racks to cool completely. Repeat with the remaining dough and trimmings.
Into a medium bowl, sift together the confectioners' sugar and cream of tartar. With an electric mixer, beat in the egg whites until well mixed; then increase the speed, and continue beating until stiff and beaters leave a clean path in bottom of bowl. If you like, divide the icing into small bowls, and add a few drops of food coloring to each portion of the icing. Add a little lemon juice or rum to achieve a spreading consistency. Spoon the icing or icings into one or more paper cones, and pipe decorations onto the gingerbread people. Allow to dry 2 hours at room temperature. Store in airtight containers.

Acknowledgments

The Publishers would like to thank Kay Quigley, Darren Braithwaite, and Liz Day of Schwartz, McCormick UK Ltd, Haddenham, Buckinghamshire, England, for advice and help in the supply of the vast majority of spices photographed for this book. We would also like to thank Joseph Flach of Peterborough, England, and Fox's Spices of Stratford upon Avon, Warwickshire, England, for advice and the supply of some of the more unusual spices (Fox's Spices are available by mail order on Tel: (00 44) 1789 266420, Fax: (00 44) 1789 267737).

Picture Credits

Key *b* = bottom, *l* = left, *m* = middle, *r* = right, *t* = top

p3: JA Sharwood & Co Ltd; p7: JA Sharwood & Co Ltd; p8: ET Archive; p9: JA Sharwood & Co Ltd; p12: Seasoning & Spice Association; p15: Quarto Publishing: p25, *tl*: Quarto Publishing; p52, *bl*, p54, *bl*, p55, *ml*, *mr*, p 56, *bl*, p 59, p61, p63, *m*, p66, *b*, p69, p72, *b*, p74, *t*, p76, *t*, p81, *tl*, p83, *b*, p85, *b*, p87, *tr*, p89, *t*, p90, p92, *m*, p95, *b*, p96, *t*, p97, *b*, p98, *m*, p100, p101, *t*, p102, p103, *r*, p108, *t*, p109, p112, *b*, p113, *t*, p114, *t*, p115, *m*, p117, *m*, p118, *b*, p119, *b*, p122, *t*, p123, *br*: A-Z Botanical Collection Ltd.